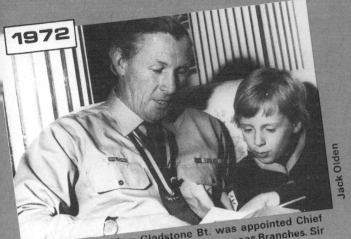

1972

Jack Olden

In July, Sir William Gladstone Bt. was appointed Chief Scout of the United Kingdom and Overseas Branches. Sir William, shown here with his son Charles (who was then in the Cubs) has since visited most parts of the country.

the CUB SCOUT

annual 1980

Scouts

The Official Annual of The Scout Association

Edited by David Harwood

1975

Jack Olden

17,700 Scouts from 94 countries met in Lillehammer, Norway, for the 14th World Jamboree. NORDJAMB '75, as it was called, was hosted by the five Nordic countries. A computer was used to sort everybody into the 1,500 Patrols so that there was not more than one person from any one country in a Patrol!

1979

Alan Vince

'Cub Country' was the code name for the project the Cub Scout Section undertook in this year. The country was Nepal, one of the poorest countries in the world, and during the year Cubs raised money to help Nepalese Cubs and Scouts educate their villages in ways of producing more food and improving their health.

1978

Andrew Pearson

The 1978 Cub Adventure Days were held at the Norfolk County Show Ground. More than 1,600 Cub Scouts took part in the four-day event.

Now we're going into the 1980s . . . with lots of exciting things in store!

Contents

253005

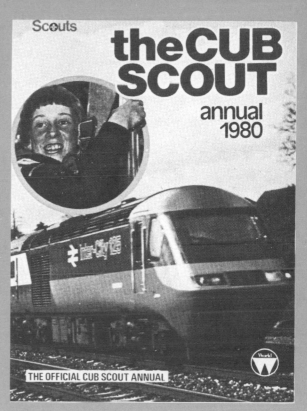

THE COVER PHOTOGRAPHS

Graham Sharman of Frampton Cotterell in Avon sums up all the fun and excitement of being a Cub Scout at the Dodington Adventure Playground . . . And there was certainly lots of fun and excitement for some Cub Scouts when they became High Speed Cub Scouts on British Rail's Inter-City 125 train: you can read about their adventures inside.

photographs by David Harwood and British Transport Films

Copyright © MCMLXXIX by The Scout Association. All rights reserved throughout the world.

Published in Great Britain by World Distributors (Manchester) Limited, A Pentos Company, P.O. Box 111, 12 Lever Street, Manchester M60 1TS. Printed in Great Britain by Morrison & Gibb Ltd., Edinburgh SBN 7235 6533 3

WORLD & WHITMAN

This Annual belongs to:

CROSSWORD FOOD, GLORIOUS FOOD

by Daphne Pilcher

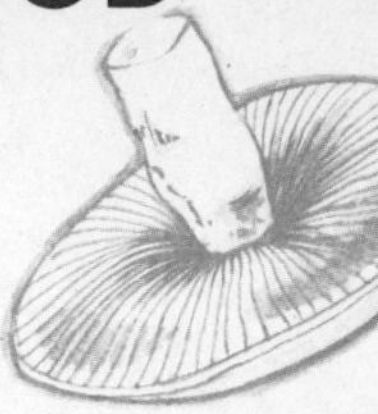

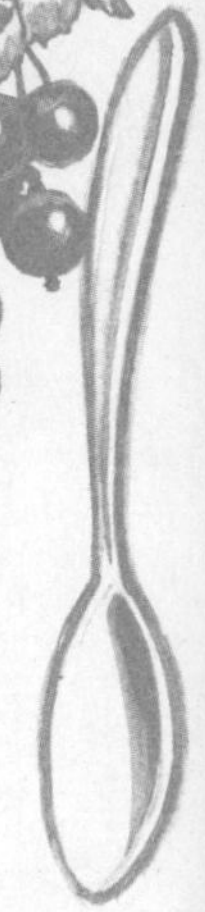

CLUES ACROSS:

1. Give a mouse another S and get a kind of sweet (6).
5. A fish often eaten with chips (6).
7. What a hen lays (3).
9. Stands holding salt, pepper and mustard (6).
11. Apples, pears, strawberries are all this (5).
13. You can find this drink in chocolate (5).
15. These are nice for tea, especially iced or with cream (5).
18. You have this kind of beef with Yorkshire pudding (5).
21. Freshwater fish, sometimes rainbow, eaten grilled (5).
22. Wooden potatoes? (5).
23. A piece of cutlery (5).
26. A slice of bacon (6).
29. 'Four and twenty blackbirds baked in a ___' (3).
30. A sniff of this will make you sneeze (6).
31. A monkey likes this fruit (6).

CLUES DOWN:

1. Anagram of lemon produces a rather exotic fruit (5).
2. A spoonful of this helps the medicine go down (5).
3. A mixed up lump creates a fruit (4).
4. One of the things made by the Queen of Hearts (4).
6. This vegetable is supposed to make you see in the dark (6).
8. Part of the body (5).
10. A tinned fish, pink or red, often eaten with salad (6).
12. A slice of 'grilled' bread (5).
14. Made from milk and spread on your bread (6).
15. This fish has the initial letters of Cash on Delivery (3).
16. Tomato, oxtail, lentil and chicken are all types of these (5).
17. When a plate is hot this protects the table (3).
19. North of England dish eaten with onions (5).
20. Mouse food? (6).
24. This vegetable brings tears to your eyes (5).
25. Sauce covering peaches or thin crisp toast (5).
27. Juice of a lemon (4).
28. Cattle meat (4).

Solution on page 63.

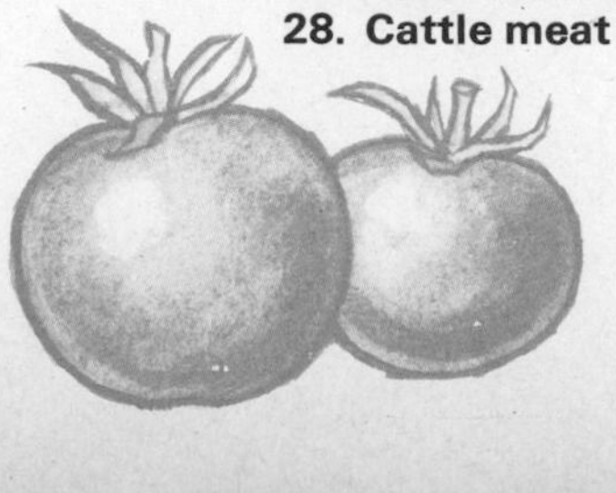

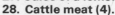

Make yourself a WATER BOMB

by ERIC FRANKLIN

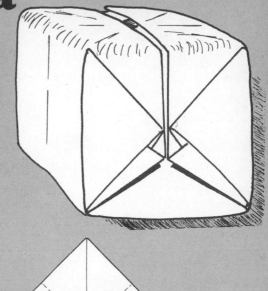

Here is a nice gadget with which you can have some fun. The Water Bomb is of Japanese origin and can be found in many books of Origami, the Japanese art of paper folding. When made, it can actually be filled with water. Alternatively, you could make a number of them, fill each with water and have a battle royal at camp, using them as water bombs! Less violently you can make them with coloured paper and use them for Christmas decorations (but don't fill them with water!).

You will need a piece of paper about six inches (150 mm) square – and it must be a true square. Thin notepaper, or bank paper, is suitable but, in fact, almost any paper can be used.

Here are the instructions:

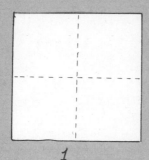

Fold the paper in half in both directions and crease well.

1

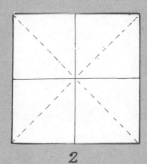

Turn the paper over and fold diagonally in both directions.

2

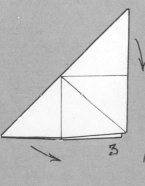

Hold the folded corners between the fingers and thumbs and push inwards towards the point. This will give you the familiar dart flight.

3

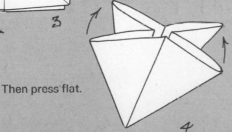

Then press flat.

4

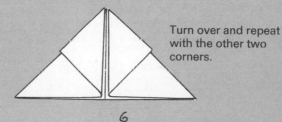

5 Press down firmly and then fold the corners up to the centre point.

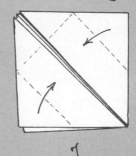

Turn over and repeat with the other two corners.

6

Fold the outer corners to the centre and then fold the top points down, as indicated by the dotted lines. Turn over and repeat on the other side.

7

Fold the two small upper corners down into the little pockets just below them. Turn over and do the same on the reverse side. Press all the folds down firmly and then, holding lightly, inflate by blowing into the small hole at the base as indicated by the arrow in Fig. 8.

You have now made a Japanese Water Bomb and I hope you have lots of fun with it.

8

HIGH SPEED
CUB SCOUTS

Getting the Power

253008

Part 1

Words: David Harwood **Photographs: David Stower** (British Transport Films)

On Monday 4th October 1976 a new chapter in railway history began when the fastest diesel train in the world – British Rail's 'Inter-City 125' – came into service on the Western Region between London, Bristol and South Wales. Some eighteen months later, on 8th May 1978, the first six of Eastern Region's High Speed Trains started passenger carrying journeys on the East Coast main line linking London with Yorkshire, the North East and Scotland. In May 1979 a full service with thirty-two trains started on the East Coast main line.

What's the story behind these super-sleek rockets of the iron road? How and where are they built? What's it feel like to speed along at 125 mph? British Rail allowed a few Cub Scouts to go behind the scenes to find out for the CUB SCOUT ANNUAL.

It was one of the few really hot days of June 1978. Richard Neil and Russell Dale of the Whiteleaf Pack, Princes Risborough, Buckinghamshire, and Philip Barratt and Jonathan Garside of the 125th Derby made their ways to Crewe. I travelled from my home in Bristol. By a masterpiece of organisation, John Fogg, British Rail's Information Officer, got everyone – including the boys' Leaders and the photographer – to Crewe within a few minutes of each other.

We were driven to British Rail Engineering's Crewe Works where we met Mr. Frank Merrill, a Training Assistant in the Works, who was to be our guide for the day. We went to the Board Room. Mr. Merrill showed the boys a model of the Works so they would know where they would be going. Soon the Cubs were asking questions, so I'll let them take up the story. . . .

How long have trains been made here?

A long time! The works started production for the Grand Junction Railway in 1843. Since then it's grown enormously . . .

When was the last steam train built?

The last one from these works was finished in December 1958. We started making diesel locomotives and later electric locomotives. Our main job now is repairing and maintaining all sorts of locomotives . . .

What about the High Speed Train?

The prototype was made at Crewe and started trial running in 1972. We made the first production power unit in 1975.

Is all the train built here?

No. The passenger coaches, restaurant and buffet cars are built by British Rail Engineering at Derby. We make the two power units for each High Speed Train.

Does each train have two engines, then?

Remember we call them power cars. But yes, there is an 'engine' at each end.

Why's that?

They give the train the power needed to accelerate quickly, and it makes the operation of the train much simpler. An HST can go into a terminal, and all a driver has to do is to drive the train from the other end when it's taken out again. Also, *if* one of the power units develops a fault, the other one is still powerful enough to pull – or push – the train at up to 100 mph. I think it's high time we went and saw how the power units are made. Let's go into the works.

Boys and Leaders looking at a model of the Crewe works.

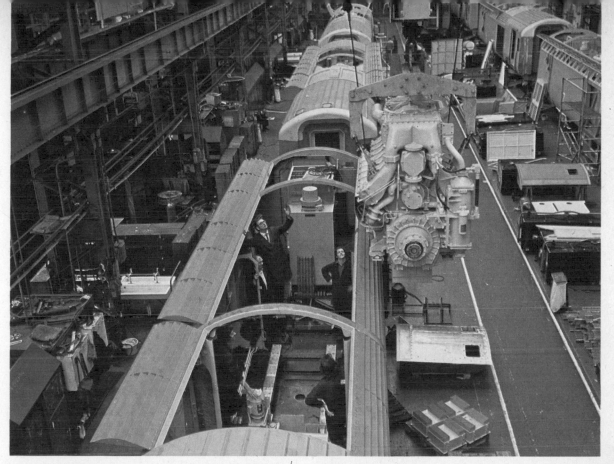

How is a power car built?

Basically in three parts – the underframe, the body and the bogies. Here you can see the bodyframe being welded onto the underframe. This shell will then have the side and roof sections put on, and will be fitted out with all its equipment. The bogies are fitted last as complete units.

What engine does it have?

It's a 2,250 horse-power Ruston Paxman Valenta, made by G.E.C. Diesels Ltd. There are 12 cylinders – six on either side – set in a vee form.

What's the driver's cab made from?

Reinforced glass fibre, 50 mm thick. It's very tough so the driver is fully protected.

How strong is the windscreen when it's fitted?

Very strong indeed. It's made out of laminated high-impact resistant safety glass.

What huge springs!

They'll be fitted to a bogie. Each bogie has four springs.

Why is the bodywork such peculiar colours?
It's just been undercoated – you'll see more about the paintwork in the paint shop.

Why is the front shaped like that?
It reduces the wind resistance when the train's travelling at high speed.

Where are the buffers?
Go and have a look! They're underneath. You'll also see the emergency coupling where the emergency towing gear can be fixed.

This is the paint shop.

How many coats does each unit have?
Nine altogether, and the top coats are all hand painted.

How long does it take to build a power car?
About ten weeks, and we aim to complete about two power units each week – a pair went out just before you arrived this morning.

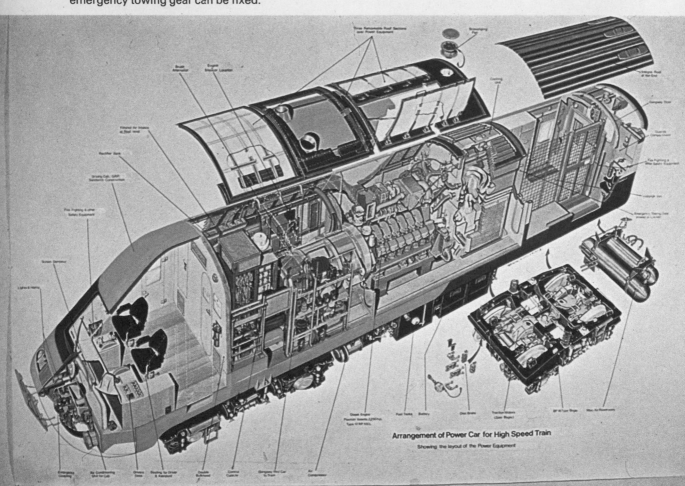

Arrangement of Power Car for High Speed Train
Showing the layout of the Power Equipment

A cutaway drawing of the 125's Power Unit, by courtesy of British Rail

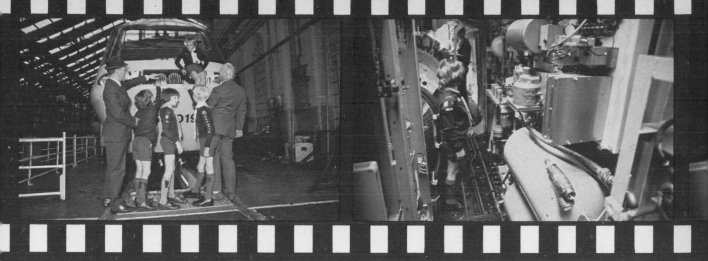

With Works Superintendant Reg Partridge (left), the boys inspected the front of the power unit which would be completed the following week. But there was more to come. . . .

They were allowed to have a good look inside the 'engine room' . . .

How many miles to the gallon does it do?
A train with two power cars and seven carriages needs about 1.3 gallons of fuel for each mile at top speed.

How far can it go without re-fuelling?
Up to 1,100 miles. The fuel tank will hold 1,000 gallons.

. . . into the driver's cab to have a feel of the controls . . .

. . . and down into the pit to look underneath . . .

How heavy is it?
Each power unit weighs 66 tonnes, and each carriage weighs between 33 and 39 tonnes.

How much does it cost?
A pair of power units would cost about one million pounds!

It had been a long day, though the boys had had a break at mid-day when they were entertained to lunch. They returned to the Board Room where they met Mr. Frank de Nobriga, the Works Manager. They were pleasantly surprised when he told them he had been in Scouting as a boy.

It was time to go. The Cubs went to the station and went their separate ways . . . but it wouldn't be long before they met again for the second part of their High Speed Train adventure. You can read about that on page 54.

THE CUB SCOUT ANNUAL gratefully acknowledges the assistance of British Rail, without whose co-operation this feature would not have been possible.

Indians of North America

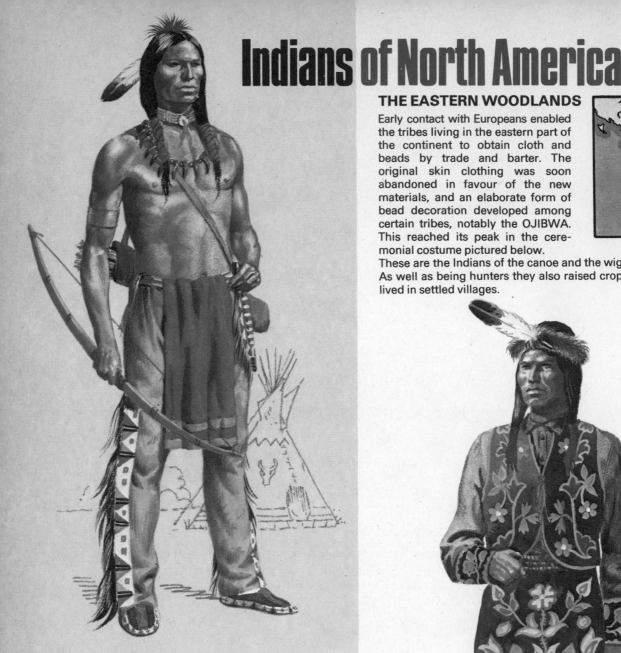

THE EASTERN WOODLANDS

Early contact with Europeans enabled the tribes living in the eastern part of the continent to obtain cloth and beads by trade and barter. The original skin clothing was soon abandoned in favour of the new materials, and an elaborate form of bead decoration developed among certain tribes, notably the OJIBWA. This reached its peak in the ceremonial costume pictured below.

These are the Indians of the canoe and the wigwam. As well as being hunters they also raised crops and lived in settled villages.

THE GREAT PLAINS

Between the Rocky Mountains in the west and the rivers and forests of the eastern United States lie the great plains, or prairies. This area was the home of the Plains Indians, the buffalo hunting tribes. They are undoubtedly the best known of all Indians, the most notable tribes of which are the SIOUX, CHEYENNE, BLACKFOOT, CROW, ARAPAHO, PAWNEE, KIOWA and COMANCHE. They led a nomadic life, following the great herds of buffalo upon which they depended for their subsistence. Their normal dress was breech cloth, leggings, and moccasins, with a buffalo robe or blanket for the upper half. The feather war-bonnet and decorated buckskin shirt was only worn on special occasions.

written and illustrated by Frank Humphris

THE SOUTH WEST

Among the many tribes living in the hot dry country of the south west, the best known and most numerous were the NAVAJOS and the APACHES. Unlike the peaceful PUEBLO, HOPI and other tribes of the region that were famous for their arts and crafts, war was a way of life to the Navajo and Apache. The Navajo were subdued in 1868 by the U.S. army since when they have lived on their reservation in peace, but the Apache carried on fighting and it was not until 1886 that Geronimo, their last fighting chief, surrendered. For dwellings they used both the tepee and the 'wickeyup', a shelter made of brushwood and grass over a framework of poles.

THE NORTH WEST COAST

Along the north west Pacific coast of America dwelt the tribes that are famous for their splendid wood carving. They have strange sounding names – TLINGIT, KWAKIUTL, HAIDA, TSIMSHIAN, NOOTKA, etc. and they are best known to us through their great totem poles. These are a notable feature of the area. Some reach a height of sixty feet, and were erected as memorials to chiefs, or portrayed the owner's family crest, or featured some mythological event. They also built large sea-going canoes, their main diet being fish – they even hunted the whale. The prevailing wet climate led them to develop permanent houses built of wood, which were often richly carved and decorated.

DOWN ON THE FARM

devised and drawn by Peter Harrison

Not many years ago 8 or 9 men were employed on a dairy farm doing the work which, with modern machinery and methods, can now be done by just one man.

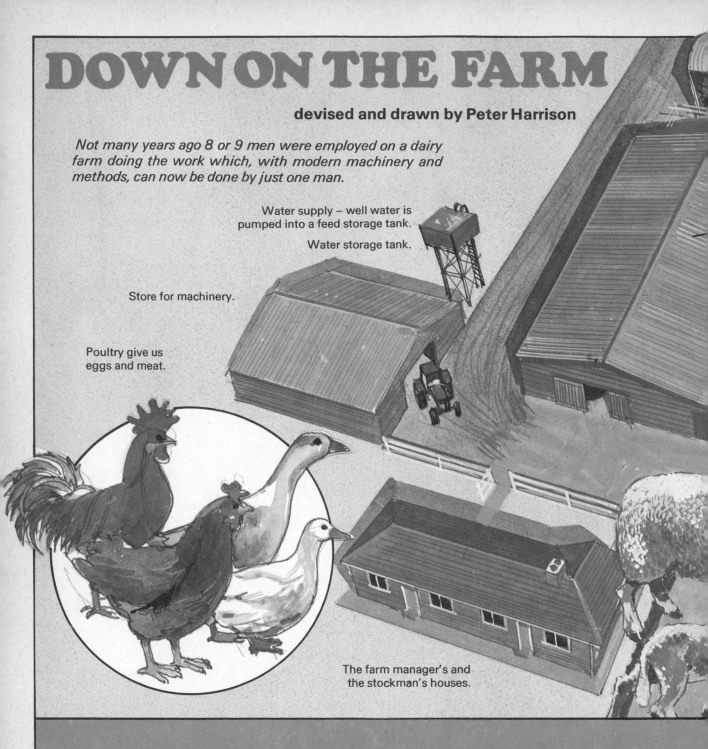

Water supply – well water is pumped into a feed storage tank.

Water storage tank.

Store for machinery.

Poultry give us eggs and meat.

The farm manager's and the stockman's houses.

Although thousands of acres each year are taken for the growth of towns and cities, more than two-thirds of Britain's land is farmed. It's the farmers' task to produce as much food as possible for us to eat, so that we do not have to buy more than is necessary from other countries.

Arable farms are those on which root crops and cereals are grown.

Dairy farms 'specialise' in milk production – there are about 3,500,000 dairy cows in Great Britain.

Mixed farms are those which have a dairy herd and grow various crops as well. Many farms also raise cattle for their meat. This bird's eye view shows that a farm of the 1980s is a highly efficient business.

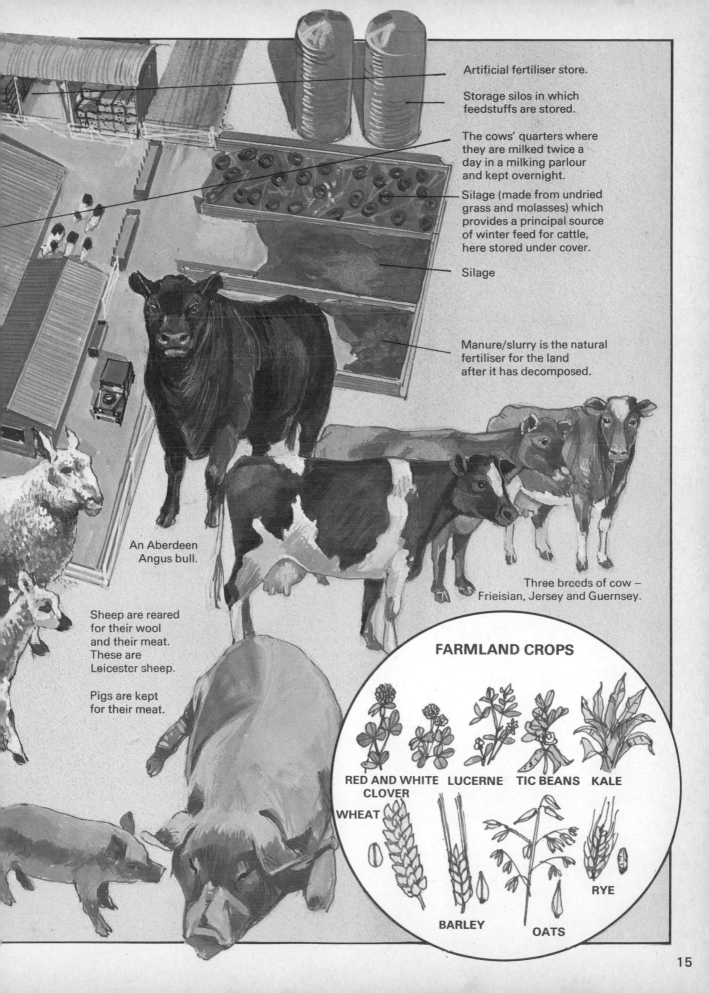

Artificial fertiliser store.

Storage silos in which feedstuffs are stored.

The cows' quarters where they are milked twice a day in a milking parlour and kept overnight.

Silage (made from undried grass and molasses) which provides a principal source of winter feed for cattle, here stored under cover.

Silage

Manure/slurry is the natural fertiliser for the land after it has decomposed.

An Aberdeen Angus bull.

Three breeds of cow – Frieisian, Jersey and Guernsey.

Sheep are reared for their wool and their meat. These are Leicester sheep.

Pigs are kept for their meat.

FARMLAND CROPS

RED AND WHITE CLOVER

LUCERNE

TIC BEANS

KALE

WHEAT

BARLEY

OATS

RYE

Farm Machinery

by Peter Harrison

Little more than 100 years ago, more people worked on the land than in any other occupation. Nowadays farm machinery enables one man to do the work of many. Here you can see just a few of the farmers' 'tools'. Find out more from books in your school or local public library. Visit a farm with your family or your Pack... but remember, NEVER play on farm machinery: it can be dangerous and it is **expensive**.

MOWERS are used to cut grass to make hay. The fast moving knives are powered by the tractor's engine via the power-take-off (PTO) shaft. The tractor is the farmer's most versatile machine.

THE REVERSIBLE PLOUGH is double sided and can be turned at the end of each row so that a field can be ploughed from one side to the other instead of in separate sections.

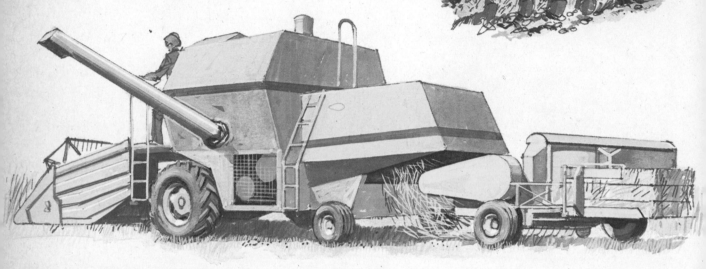

THE COMBINE HARVESTER cuts and threshes corn, stores the grain, and deposits the straw behind. The straw is then picked up by a BALER in which it is compressed, wired and ejected.

THE FORAGE HARVESTER gathers green crops for silage. The flails turn very fast, cutting and chopping the crop and creating a draught which blows the greenery into a trailer pulled by another tractor.

A HAY TEDDER is mounted behind a tractor to turn and toss grass which has been cut for hay so that air gets into it and it dries more quickly.

THE COMBINE DRILL is pulled by a tractor. It cuts furrows, plants seed, feeds fertiliser and covers the seed in a single operation.

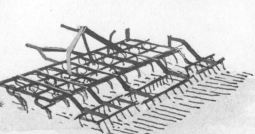

THE CULTIVATOR with its spike-like tines breaks up the soil before crops are planted. A cultivator can have either rigid tines or spring tines.

St.George for Scouting

by Vic Clapham

April 23rd is St. George's Day

Baden-Powell selected St. George as Patron Saint of all Scouts everywhere, not because he also happened to be Patron Saint of England, but because he was Patron Saint of Chivalry throughout Europe, and was revered in both Christian and Islamic circles and by many others. B.-P. chose him because St. George exemplified devotion, piety, courage, leadership, truthfulness and dedication. St. George is symbolic of Scout ideals.

It is believed that St. George was born in Cappadocia, Asia Minor. He rose to high rank in the Roman cavalry, and lived during the time of the Roman Emperor, Diocletian – A.D. 245 to 313. When Diocletian ordered a persecution of the Christians, St. George chose death rather than carry out the order, and was cruelly put to death on April 23rd, A.D. 303.

In A.D. 494 St. George was canonised by Pope Gelasius who said he was one of those "whose names are justly reverenced among men, but whose acts are known only to God".

The Spirit Of Sheikh Kedir

On the slopes of Mount Hermon there's a tiny Arab village, Banias, standing on the ruins of the ancient Greek city of Paneas, later known as Caesarea Philippi – which Jesus knew – and still later, under the reign of Nero, it was called Neroneas.

At Banias there's a grotto. Here the River Jordan begins. Near the grotto is the small, white-domed shrine of Sheikh Kedir, legendary Arab prophet. Centuries before the birth of Muhammad the Arabs believed – and still believe – that the spirit of Sheikh Kedir entered the body of St. George and inspired his great deeds. With the coming of Muhammad this veneration of St. George was extended to all followers of the Islamic faith.

Then came the Crusades. Everywhere the Crusaders went they heard

PATRON SAINT OF ALL SCOUTS

stories from the Arabs, of the courage, chivalry and holiness of St. George. Richard the Lion Heart, King of England, was so impressed that, after restoring the Church of St. George at Lydda, he returned home with the cry: "St. George for England".

The legend of St. George and the Dragon is, of course, an allegorical expression of the triumph of good over evil. The legend tells of how he rode into the city of Sylene, in present-day Libya, where he learned of a dragon that was fed daily with one of the citizens. This day the victim was to be the king's daughter, Cleolinda. St. George saved her by killing the dragon.

Thus, the Patron Saint of Scouts everywhere was and is revered by many peoples, of different religious beliefs, in many lands. Venerated throughout Arabia as an incarnation of Sheikh Kedir, revered as a holy man by the followers of Islam, and immortalised as a Christian Saint, this officer of ancient Rome is today the universal symbol of a chivalrous, courageous way of life to millions of Scouts of all races and creeds.

Lord Baden-Powell, the Founder of Scouting, was a talented artist. This is one of his sketches illustrating how he expects young people, through Scouting, to face difficulties and disappointments with courage.

Make your own
CRYSTAL RECEIVER

by Neil Lucas

Two Cub Scouts with their home – made crystal receiver

Parts you will need:

1 tin can, 70 mm dia. (2¾")
1 tin can, 76 mm dia. (3")
350 cm of 36 s.w.g. enamelled copper wire for coil.
A diode – OA90
Crystal earpiece
Wooden baseboard, 15 x 10 cm
A 7 cm square of thin card or a 1 cm diameter cardboard tube
Four screws with metal cup washers
Earth wire, as required
7 –10 metres of aerial wire
Sellotape
Plasticine
Connecting wire – 50 cm thin insulated wire

BASEBOARD DETAILS

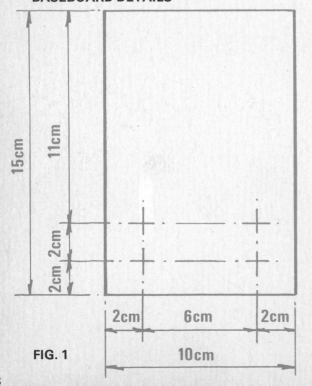

15cm
11cm
2cm 2cm
2cm
2cm 6cm 2cm
10cm

FIG. 1

ASSEMBLY INSTRUCTIONS

A. THE TUNING CAPACITOR

1. Completely cover the outside of the *small* can with Sellotape.
2. Attach approximately 25 cm of connecting wire to the end of each can by soldering or by making a *small* hole in the end of each can and securing the wires to the inside of each can with plasticine.
3. Place the smaller can inside the larger can.

B. THE COIL

1. Roll the 7 cm square of card into a 1 cm diameter tube *or* use a 1 cm diameter cardboard tube.
2. Leaving approximately 10 cm at each end, wind the enamelled wire 100 times closely round the 1 cm tube.
3. Secure the wire to the tube with sellotape (leaving ends for connection).
4. Using fine sandpaper, remove enamel from the ends of the coil wire to ensure good contact.

LAYOUT AND DIAGRAM OF THE CRYSTAL RECEIVER

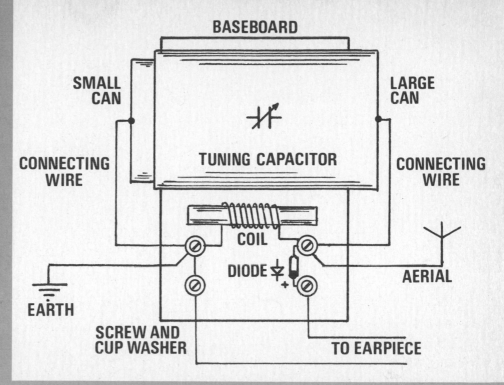

FIG. 2

C. THE BASEBOARD
1. Mark out baseboard as shown in Fig. 1
2. Fit the cup washers to screws and secure to baseboard (see Fig. 2)

D. PUTTING THE PARTS TOGETHER
Assemble the components as shown in Figs. 2, 3 and 4.
Notes (1) The diode must be inserted as shown in the diagram, with the cathode (the end with a red spot) towards the earpiece.
(2) Secure the tins to the baseboard with plasticine.

OPERATING INSTRUCTIONS

1. Attach earth wire to water tap.
2. Suspend the aerial wire as high as possible.
3. With earpiece fitted, slowly move the small can in and out of the larger one until a radio programme can be heard clearly.

FIG. 3

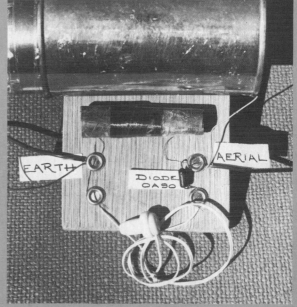

FIG. 4

by Cliff Brown

HOW WELL DO YOU KNOW YOUR ROAD SIGNS?

THE PHANTOM ROAD SIGN PAINTER HAS BEEN AT WORK! SOME OF THE ROAD SIGNS BELOW ARE FAKES! DO YOU KNOW WHICH ARE GENUINE AND WHAT THEY MEAN? (THERE'S A BONUS TOO – IF YOU KNOW WHAT THE FAKE ONES ARE!)

RHYMING PAIRS PUZZLE!

TAKE A LONG LOOK AT THE EIGHT PICTURES BELOW AND TRY TO PUT THEM TOGETHER AS FOUR 'RHYMING PAIRS'!

SPOT THE DIFFERENCES

IF YOU'VE GOT A REALLY KEEN EYE FOR DETAIL, STUDY THE TWO PICTURES BELOW – THEY MAY LOOK THE SAME, BUT THERE ARE A NUMBER OF DIFFERENCES.
(HOW MANY CAN YOU SPOT?)

Answers on page 63

20

Make the most of your Camera

words and pictures by Bill Carden (Fellow of the Royal Photographic Society)

I expect you always look forward to collecting your photographs after they have been processed. You hope there will be some good, interesting pictures which you cannot wait to show to your friends. But what often happens? As you look through the prints for the first time, excitement gives way to disappointment. There are wobbly ones, dark ones, light ones... you know what I mean.

Problems

Mistakes are expensive in photography. You can avoid making the same mistakes again and again if you know how your camera works and understand its capabilities. So let's look at some of the problems and how they can be solved.

1. Whatever camera you have, always read the instructions which came with the camera and learn to handle the controls.

2. Develop a mental checklist before you use the camera so you will not put part of your hand or the camera case in front of the lens, or forget to take off the lens cap, or shoot without a film.

3. Probably more pictures are ruined by an unsteady hand than by any other single cause. Unless you are shooting at high shutter speeds even a slight shake or jiggle when you click the shutter will result in some loss of sharpness, if not actual blurring. It is essential to hold the camera very still at the moment of taking, especially with speeds as low as 1/30th second used on simple cameras. On cameras with a shutter speed control, use as high a speed as possible.

4. Many failures have exposure problems. While an inexpensive camera can take good pictures in ordinary daylight, it cannot do so in low-lighting conditions. An exposure meter will help, but you will achieve more if you always use a film with the same 'rating' or 'speed'. With increasing skill you will remember exposures in varying light conditions. It's a good idea when you're a beginner to keep a few notes.

SWAN – taken in a Wild Life Park – a feeling of Spring! Whatever you do – move in close and fill the frame. Side lighting is most effective and the dark background does not distract. Unless you have a more expensive camera and use a lens hood it will be dangerous to point towards the sun. At the same time to place the sun behind your shoulders will make unexciting pictures and your subjects will not like looking directly into the sun.

Camera Controls

Let's now consider a camera's basic controls and their purpose. Perhaps you have a camera with a focussing control, a shutter to adjust the speed, and a fixed lens marked with what are known as F numbers which adjust the size of the aperture.

The basic operation of the shutter is to control light and motion. I've advised you to use a fast shutter speed and for those normal shots it is as well to set the shutter at 1/125th second even before you leave the house. This speed will help to 'freeze' the subject and improve the sharpness of your pictures. Speeds set at less than 1/30th second require the use of a tripod, or the camera must be braced securely on a fence or any solid base or upright.

There will always be exceptions, and it is possible to use a slow shutter speed to create blurr intentionally: often most success will be achieved by roughly focussing and following the action in the viewfinder.

This is often referred to as 'panning'. The background will be blurred but the subject remains reasonably sharp. Similar effects can be achieved with faster shutter speeds, but the background will show less blur.

By adjustment of the F numbers the aperture can also control light and have an effect upon focus, often referred to as 'depth of field'. What happens is more easy to understand if you remember that the smaller the aperture, the more the foreground and the background will be in focus.

Looking for Pictures

So much for the technical side of handling the camera. It can be said that the camera is only the tool to be used as an extension of your eyes and hands. It is possible to use the shutter and aperture controls together, and creatively to make your pictures more interesting. A sound technique is essential. It must be acquired. But the real fun is looking for pictures in

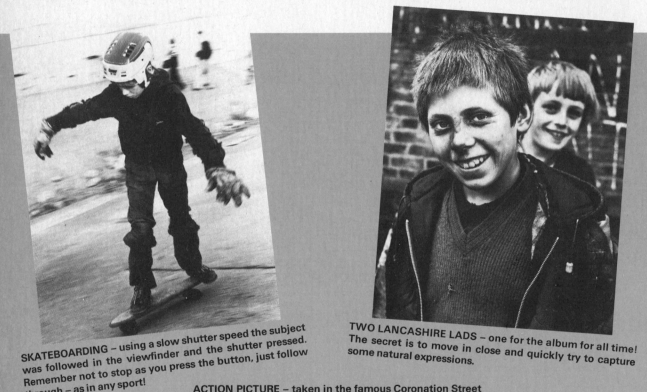

SKATEBOARDING – using a slow shutter speed the subject was followed in the viewfinder and the shutter pressed. Remember not to stop as you press the button, just follow through – as in any sport!

TWO LANCASHIRE LADS – one for the album for all time! The secret is to move in close and quickly try to capture some natural expressions.

ACTION PICTURE – taken in the famous Coronation Street in Salford and close to the Manchester United Football Ground. Here the subjects were followed in the viewfinder and a series of pictures were taken. Notice the side lighting and again the dark background.

the viewfinder and an enthusiastic young person like you will not be lacking in ideas!

Sadly, even at this stage – at the moment of taking a picture – many more mistakes are made.

Are you close enough to the subject? Move in close! Be adventurous! Completely fill the viewfinder with your picture, trying not to include anything unnecessary.

What's in the background? A common error when photographing people is to include distracting or unwanted backgrounds. The best way with a portrait is to move in close and point down – but also remember my earlier advice to use a fast shutter speed and a wide aperture to reduce the area of focus.

Will the vertical lines of buildings be distorted? This error is easily cured by holding the camera level. The distortion will then be corrected and any sloping horizontals removed.

Attacking the Subject

The real secret of successful picture taking is how you 'attack' and 'feel for' your subject. First select your subject, and then become totally involved – and stay involved, always trying to select interesting moments. If possible, take a series of pictures that will tell a story. When taking people, why not involve them in an activity to help reduce the number of posed shots?

The camera can be your very special friend with a unique and magic power to capture people, animals and places. With your pictures you can communicate with other people your own very special view of the world. I hope that you'll be fired with fun and enthusiasm, and that you'll soon go out and take your next picture . . . and your *next* picture must always be your *best* picture.

It sometimes helps to look for patterns, shapes and silhouettes. It is possible to compose the picture in the viewfinder. The decision where to place the horse in the picture area must be considered. This photograph was taken in the fog – well, why not? Lighting conditions will still be suitable.

With people engage the subjects in an activity and create a happy and relaxed atmosphere.

When including buildings hold the camera level. In this picture (and in any landscape) it is useful to add some human interest in the foreground. It will also help to give scale.

LEARN WATER SENSE

RIVERS ARE DEEP AND UNSAFE FOR PADDLING AND SWIMMING

OBEY DANGER WARNING NOTICES

ALWAYS FISH WHERE THERE ARE OTHERS

CANALS HAVE STEEP SIDES - NEVER PLAY ON TOW PATHS

DO NOT TAKE INFLATABLE TOYS AND AIR BEDS ON WATER - THEY ARE DANGEROUS THEY CAN CARRY YOU OUT TO SEA

ONLY BATHE WITH YOUR PARENTS' (OR OTHER RESPONSIBLE ADULTS') PERMISSION AND WITHIN THEIR SIGHT.

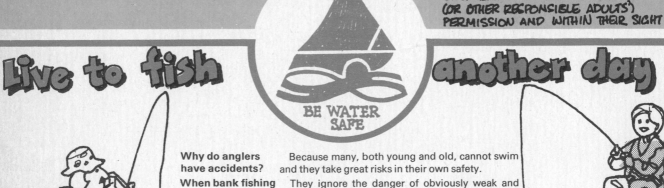

Live to fish another day

BE WATER SAFE

Why do anglers have accidents? Because many, both young and old, cannot swim and they take great risks in their own safety.

When bank fishing They ignore the danger of obviously weak and crumbling banks because they want to get as close as possible to the water.

When boat fishing A big fish is hooked, then everybody on board the boat crowds on one side to see what is coming up, and all too often the boat capsizes.

In freshwater fishing it is never necessary to stand while playing or netting a fish. It is easy to lose your balance while moving forward to drop or hoist anchor. Keep low with one hand on the gunwale.

Never wear waders or gumboots in boats. They are potential killers for not only are they difficult to get off in the water but they can hold more than enough water to drag you under.

Safety rules for sea angling Never go sea angling in a boat without a responsible adult. Make sure you know RoSPA's safety rules about boats, personal safety at sea and, or course, sea angling.

Live to fish another day By learning to swim and by wearing a lifejacket when afloat. Youngsters fishing must be watched and anglers of all ages must observe the basic safety measures.

Illustrated by Peter Harrison   Based on material from the Royal Society for the Prevention of Accidents.

An introduction to ANGLING

by
**Alan Wrangles and
Brian Robertshaw**

Angling is one of the most absorbing of all pastimes. It combines many skills, from fish identification to tying knots, as well as the very vital art of knowing how to make the best possible use of whatever tackle you have.

There are two main branches of the sport, salt (sea) and freshwater, and when buying equipment it is essential to choose that which is specially designed for the kind of angling you want to do.

Although some basic tackle arrangements and certain angling skills are common to both sea and freshwater, there are many differences between the rods, lines, weights and hooks used for the various styles of fishing.

A RIVER FLOAT FISHING ROD should be long enough to reach out over the stream so that it can guide the float tackle as it goes downstream on the current, and enable the angler to pick up line and strike fast, and so hook a taking fish. The rings guiding the line up the rod from reel to tip need to hold the fine nylon line away from the rod, because wet nylon tends to cling to the rod and thus reduce the distance light tackle can be cast.

The overall purpose of a SPINNING ROD is to cast an artificial lure. However, because the various plugs, spoons and other lures come in such an assortment of shapes and weights, rod makers have had to produce a whole range of rods to match.

Among the many other types of rods are those for beach casting, for boat fishing at sea, and a range of specialist rods for such freshwater angling styles as legering and carp fishing, and each one should be matched with the correct line.

Reels, lines, hooks and landing nets, as well as smaller items like swivels, booms, floats and bait boxes all form part of the angler's kit. You'd be wise to buy your gear from a specialist tackle shop and so be sure of obtaining expert advice.

Getting Permission

Sea fishing is free, but you should always assume when fishing in freshwater that someone owns it or controls it, and that you will have to pay. The best way to get access to freshwater fishing is to join your local angling club. Your local tackle shop will give you the name and address of the secretary.

In England and Wales you will need a Regional Water Authority Rod Licence which entitles you to use a rod and line BUT you will also need permission to actually fish in a particular stretch of water. In Scotland and Northern Ireland other rules apply but always get local advice. Wherever you are, respect private land and assume that you need to get permission to fish.

FRESHWATER FISHING

Knowing where and when to fish brings more success than just using costly tackle as, contrary to common belief, fish are not equally distributed.

The different species need the right amount of oxygen, a suitable water temperature as well as the general conditions which complement their life style. Usually, if any one or all of these factors are missing, then the species affected will move away from the area, or die.

Most rivers have a series of changing zones. If, where a stream rises the water is cold and fast flowing, trout and perhaps salmon parr (young salmon) would be the only fish. These are strong swimmers, and feed on the invertebrate animals found among stones and rocks.

Downstream, other fish such as bullhead, minnow and stoneloach might be found. The bullhead has a body which is compressed downwards making it possible for it to shelter from the main force of the current under stones and in crevices.

As the river becomes less torrential, other species join the growing assortment of both animal and plant life. In this zone species such as barbel, dace, chub and grayling may be found. These are active swimmers with well streamlined bodies. Some water plants will now be able to root in the sand and mud deposited by the slackening current.

However, there are those species which cannot live in areas where the current is swift, and the bottom mainly hard. Bream, carp and tench like a soft muddy bed with little or no flow at all. In a river they favour bays or deep hollows which give shelter during flood conditions.

Here, rushes and sedges, lily pads and other emergent plants will thrive, and the contrast between the highland and lowland stream will be most noticeable.

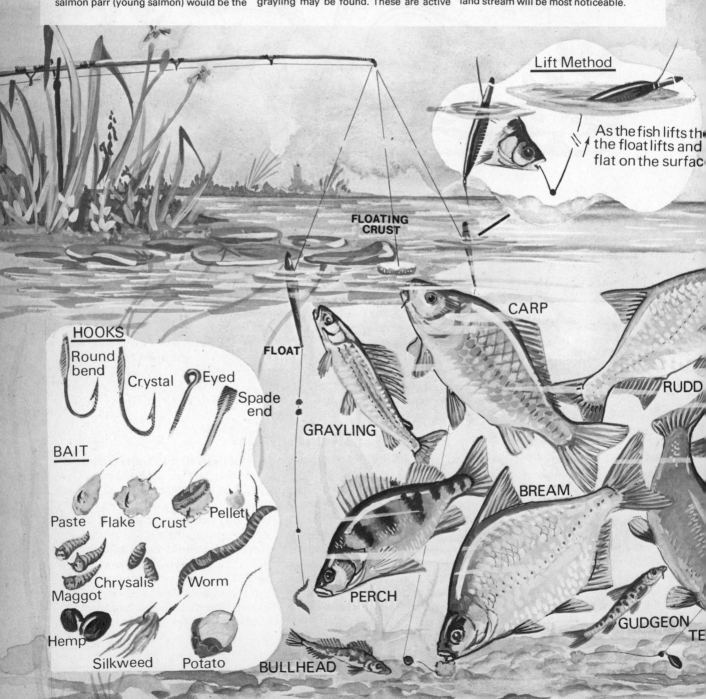

Lift Method

As the fish lifts th the float lifts and flat on the surfac

FLOATING CRUST

FLOAT

HOOKS
Round bend
Crystal
Eyed
Spade end

BAIT
Paste
Flake
Crust
Pellet
Maggot
Chrysalis
Worm
Hemp
Silkweed
Potato

GRAYLING

CARP

RUDD

PERCH

BREAM

BULLHEAD

GUDGEON

TE

Not every river has all the features which have been mentioned, some are similar from beginning to end. However, it can be assumed that wherever rivers have comparable gradients, depth, width, and the water is of a like quality, then fish stocks will be similar.

By knowing about the ways of fish, the angler can form a very good idea of the manner in which the different kinds generally feed.

Those in a fast current are likely to be taking food particles being washed along in the stream; therefore, a moving bait is likely to be taken. Float fishing or rolling leger tackle would perform well in this situation. Always remember that there are likely to be areas where the food collects naturally, having been swept there by the current. Look out for such spots and try to place a baited hook there.

Where the flow is minimal, bream, roach, carp, and tench will often take a bait which is either lying right on the bottom, or moving along an inch or two above it.

Float tackle rigged for 'laying-on' or just tripping along the bed are two good methods, as are any of the orthodox legering arrangements using the lightest possible weights.

When using the LIFT method, the fish lifts the bait as it feeds, and the float rises as the weight is disturbed. Strike as the float comes up.

Shoals of perch often cruise among reed and lily pads hunting for small fry. Try spinning or float tackle baited with worm, but never use a float larger than that necessary to support the bait. The resistance offered by an overlarge float will frighten a taking fish.

Both pike and zander are difficult fish to handle. The pike's teeth are needle sharp, and can inflict nasty wounds. Also, pike can weigh more than 30lb, and zander approach 20lb. Therefore, when fishing for them it is best to have an experienced angler with you.

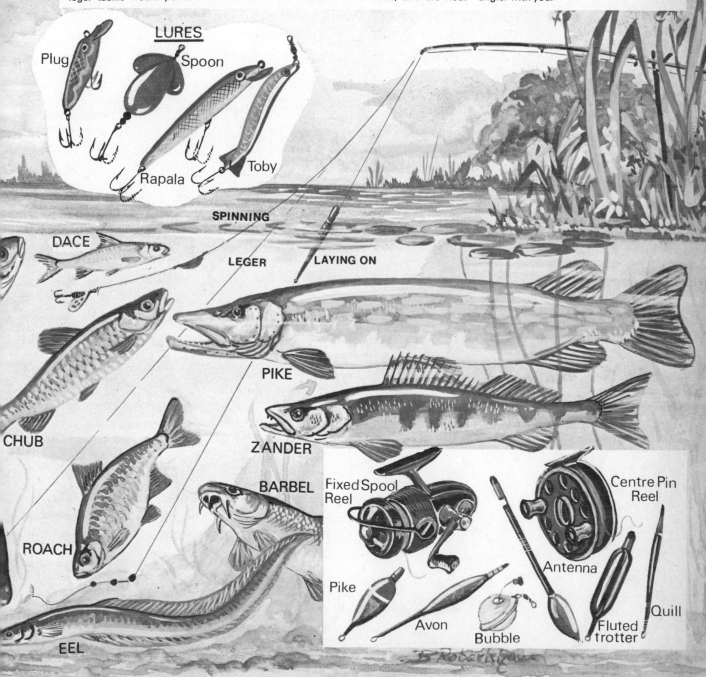

LURES

Plug

Spoon

Rapala

Toby

SPINNING

LEGER   LAYING ON

DACE

PIKE

CHUB

ZANDER

ROACH

BARBEL

Fixed Spool Reel

Centre Pin Reel

Antenna

Pike

Avon

Bubble

Fluted trotter

Quill

EEL

B. Robertson

SEA ANGLING

A vast number of species, ranging from forty foot long basking sharks to sand smelts weighing an ounce or two, live in British waters.

Some of these fish belong to families or groups which have several hundred members. For example, there are some 300 or more different sharks which belong to about 19 separate families.

Dogfish, a species often sold in fish shops as 'rock salmon' are also classed as shark, and indeed, although only weighing a few pounds, they are certainly very similar to their much larger brethren. However, even among members of the same group or family there can be widely differing habits. Some might be seasonal visitors to our shores, while others stay all year round.

For example, traditionally, beach or pier angling for cod and whiting is an autumn and winter sport, while species such as mullet, garfish, mackerel and bream are fish of the warmer months.

Also sea fish congregate in certain areas. For example, flat fish such as flounder and plaice prefer a bed of sand and mud, while other species like wrasse, pollack and ling frequent rocks and thick beds of weed. Thornback ray can be caught over shingle or sand and mud, as can gurnard and mullet.

Bass and cod are great wanderers, feeding where they can on other fish and crabs, etc. Both mackerel and garfish have similar habits, but they feed mainly on other fish and plankton.

Two words, 'demersal' and 'pelagic', are frequently used when describing the living habits of fish. Those which are 'demersal' are bottom feeders, searching for crabs, worms or other fish which live on or near the sea bed. A 'pelagic' fish swims at mid-water or close to the surface, and lives mainly on a diet of other fish,

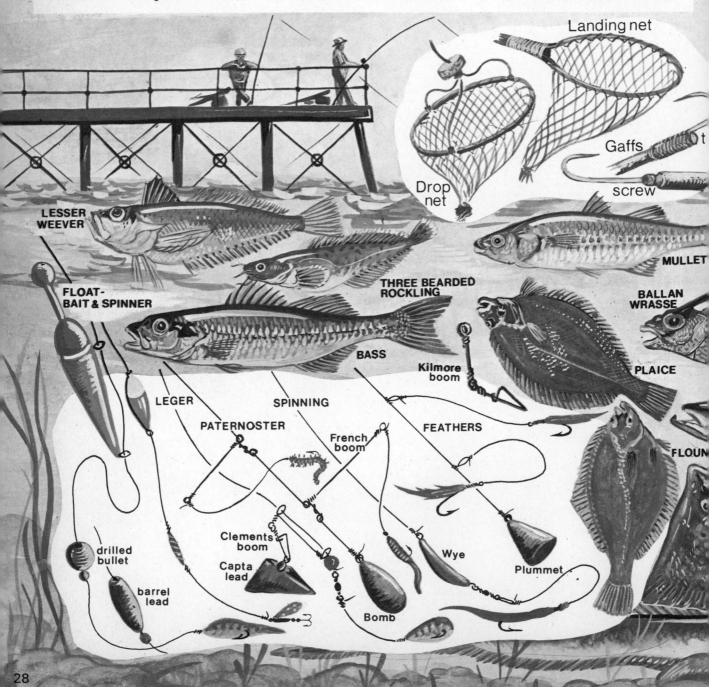

plankton and whatever items of food it can find in the upper layers of the sea.

This is not a hard and fast rule, because throughout the winter mackerel lie in huge shoals in very deep water. However, they are not bottom feeding fish in the same sense as flounders.

Mackerel are one of the easiest of fish to catch; they will snap at small spinners, hooks dressed with feathers, as well as rubber sand eels.

Keep your line moving, and every few seconds swing your rod tip so that the line of recovery is changed. This will make your line appear more like a small fish darting about, and is more likely to attract attention.

Bass and garfish will also take spinners and imitation sand eels, but bass are frequently attracted to soft or peeler crab fished on leger tackle.

Both cod and whiting feed on or near the bottom. When fishing for them try paternoster or leger tackle, size 1/0 or 2/0 Seamaster hooks baited with squid, worm, strips of fish or hermit crab.

Flounders are greatly attracted by a bait moving along the sea bed; try the baited spoon method. Cast, and then reel in slowly. This method is frequently most effective when fished with the tide flow.

Long shank thin wire hooks are best when angling for flat fish; they hold a worm bait well, and the long shank helps when removing the hook from what is usually a relatively small mouth.

Always watch out for one of the most dangerous fish in our waters – the weever. The spines are poisonous, so never handle one of these fish. Ask an adult to cut the hook free and then either bury or place it in a receptacle where it can do no more harm.

If you are ever injured by a sea fish, get proper medical attention immediately.

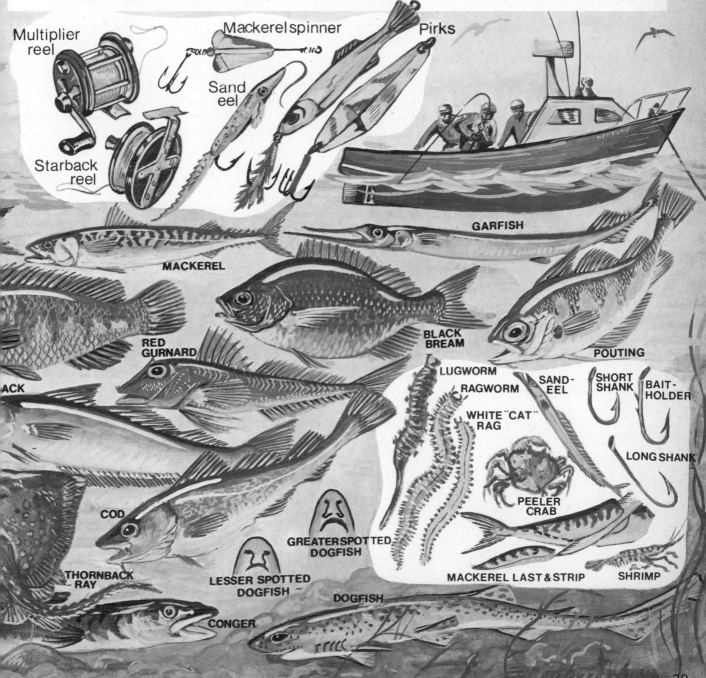

Multiplier reel

Starback reel

Mackerel spinner

Sand eel

Pirks

GARFISH

MACKEREL

RED GURNARD

BLACK BREAM

POUTING

ACK

LUGWORM

RAGWORM

WHITE "CAT" RAG

SAND-EEL

SHORT SHANK

BAIT-HOLDER

LONG SHANK

COD

PEELER CRAB

GREATER SPOTTED DOGFISH

THORNBACK RAY

LESSER SPOTTED DOGFISH

DOGFISH

MACKEREL LAST & STRIP

SHRIMP

CONGER

ROLLING OFF THE PRESSES

Up to two years before you can buy your Annual in the shops, artists, writers and photographers up and down the country are hard at work on the stories, articles and features which will appear in the book. All the material – text, photographs and artwork – has to be ready a year before publication.

The Annual's covers are printed before Christmas, and early in the New Year the Sales staff from World Distributors (our publishers) start getting orders from the booksellers. With the covers ready, they can give the shops an idea of what the book will look like.

Meanwhile, the Annual's 'inside' pages have been taking shape. The text is typeset and the pages designed to include the illustrations. All the material is then photographed. To print a colour illustration in its natural colours, only four coloured inks are used – yellow, red, blue and black. *Any* colour can be reproduced with a combination of these. A special machine 'breaks down' a colour drawing or photograph into the four basic colours, and a film for each colour is made. Thus, each 'two-colour' page has two films and each full colour page has four films. When all the films have been made these are delivered to the printers.

◀ First, the page films are assembled to make a large sheet of 32 pages.

This sheet of film is then exposed onto a light sensitive metal plate as shown in this picture (although this one is not from our Annual). ▼

It is now early summer and a decision has to be taken on how many copies of the Annual will actually be printed . . . if there are too few, a lot of you would be disappointed; if there are too many, there would be a large pile of very expensive waste paper!

This is the massive Web off-set litho printing machine on which the Annual is printed. The paper is threaded through the machine, which prints four colours on both sides of the paper one after the other. Blank paper comes off the reel and into the machine at one end, and all the inside pages of the Annual – printed and folded – come out at the other end at the rate of 10,000 Annuals an hour. When one reel of paper runs out, a new reel is automatically picked up, so that the 'web' of paper is continuous and the machine does not have to be stopped.

The covers, or cases as they are called, are made by glueing the printed covers onto squares of cardboard the size of the Annual.

The inside pages pass through this binder machine which glues the pages together at the spine, and takes them to . . .

. . . the caseing-in machine, where the inside pages and covers come together. Your Annual is now complete. However, that's not the end of the line. Copies are checked before they are packed into boxes and despatched throughout the United Kingdom and to many countries overseas.

By the time you read this – even if you got your copy on publication day in August – we'll just about have completed the 1981 Annual, and have made some plans for 1982. But if we're going to be sure that your Annual is going to be ready for you on time, we've got to be prepared!

THE CUB SCOUT ANNUAL gratefully acknowledges the co-operation of Jarrold Printing in the preparation of this feature, particularly for supplying the photographs.

When it's

by Peter Brooks

Since his very early days, man's everyday life has been governed by time. At certain times of the day he has done certain things. But man has not always had clocks and watches to tell him the time. For centuries he decided what the time was by the position of the sun in the sky, and this worked very well.

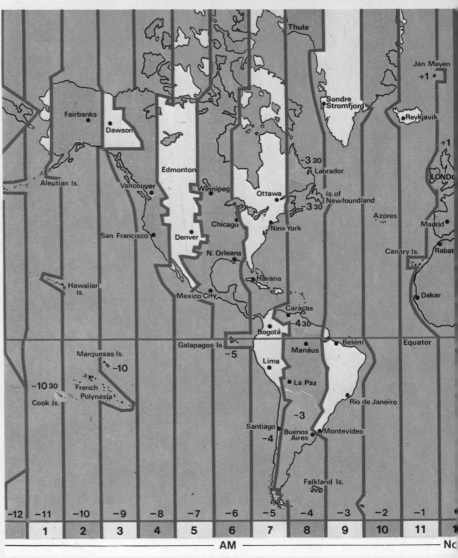

TWELVE

As people in different towns and villages saw the sun in different positions in the sky and at slightly different times, each place quickly grew to have its own 'local' time. But it was the coming of long distance railways that brought about what is known as 'Standard Time'. When the railway companies tried to draw up timetables they found it was impossible, as villages, even just 2 or 3 miles apart, each had their own time. The problems were enormous, particularly in America where, because the country was so big, it was realised that time on the east coast was several hours earlier than on the west coast.

Railway companies from 27 nations met in Washington in 1884 to try to solve the problem. Their solution was agreed and put into practice – and is still in use today.

It required that the world be divided into 24 segments (each 15° wide at the equator) and that all the places in each segment would use the same time.

They decided that Greenwich (just outside London) should be the middle and that the lines either side of Greenwich would form the middle section. Because places to the east of this saw the sun rising earlier, each of the segments would be one hour in front of the last. Thus the first would be one hour earlier than Greenwich, the second two hours, the third three and so on. And likewise the seg-

ments to the west of Greenwich would be progressively one hour later.

Of course, countries and areas did not fit neatly inside the segments so many of the lines were 'bent' so that, if they wanted, everyone could share the same time. (On the map above, the places which are in the same time

zone, as they are known, have been painted either yellow or brown and by looking at the strip across the bottom you will be able to see which section is which.)

As the line through Greenwich was the middle, and therefore assumed to be twelve o'clock (midday), there had to be a line on the other side of the world which

O'CLOCK in LONDON...

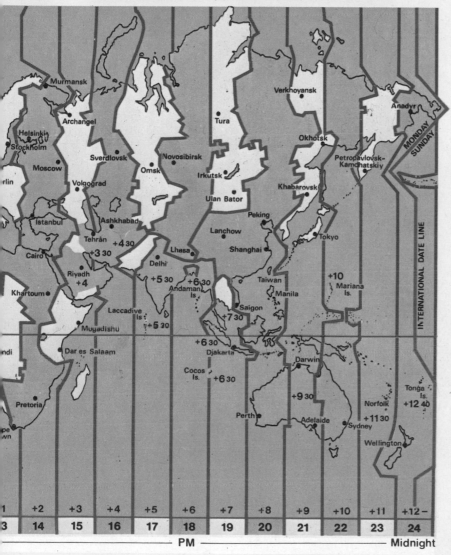

Map by Paul Tiley

It's...

12 o'clock in Paris
    Madrid & Dakar
    (same time zone)
1 pm in Berlin
    Oslo & Tripoli
2 pm in Moscow
    Khartoum & Pretoria
3 pm in Archangel
    & Riyadh
4 pm in Sverdlovsk
    & Ashkhabad
5 pm in Omsk & Delhi
6 pm in Novosibirsk
    & Lhasa
7 pm in Djakarta & Tura
8 pm in Peking,
    Shanghai & Perth
9 pm in Tokyo,
    Darwin & Adelaide
10 pm in Sydney
11 pm in Petropavlovsk-
    Kamchatskiy

And

11 am in Reykjavik
10 am in The Azores
 9 am in Rio de Janeiro
 8 am in Labrador
    & Buenos Aires
 7 am in Ottawa,
    New York & Santiago
 6 am in Winnipeg,
    Chicago & New Orleans
 5 am in Edmonton
    & Denver
 4 am in Vancouver
    & San Francisco
 3 am in Dawson
 2 am in Fairbanks
    & Hawaii
 1 am in The Cook Islands

represented midnight, and this became known as the International Date Line. On one side of it was the 'front' edge of the day and on the other side was the 'back' edge of the same day. (Imagine the map above wrapped round a ball and this will probably become clearer). Again this line was bent so that countries and islands were com-pletely on one side or the other.

To make things even more confusing, some countries introduced 'Day Time Saving' (those painted green above), this means that at certain times of the year all clocks and watches were (and still are) turned forward or back thus making the period of daylight start earlier or later.

This game, which is reproduced by courtesy of The British Gas Corporation, can be played by up to six players. Each player should have a different coloured disc. Take it in turns to spin a six-sided spinner (as illustrated) or throw a dice and see who can reach the Finish first. Work out why you can advance on some squares but have to go back or miss a turn on others . . . and then make sure you save energy about your home! Look at page 47 to find the reasons why you have to go forward or back.

34

HOW TO MAKE...

AN INDIAN WAR BONNET

**Written and illustrated
by Frank Humphris**

Only the bravest Indian warriors wore the great feather war bonnet, that most distinctive head-dress of the Plains' tribes.

For jamborees and camp fire ceremonies nothing is more impressive, yet with care and patience it can be made from materials that cost little. Large white turkey secondary wing feathers are best and you will want about forty feathers. Also a large number of the fluffy, downy feathers are required.

A

First the tips must be dyed dark brown. Shoe dye is good for this. Dip the top 2 inches in the dye, then stipple the edge with a piece of sponge to break up the straight line.

B

Each completed feather should be 13 inches long from loop to tip. If yours are short, lengthen with a piece of dowel cemented into the quill. Next cement and bind a strip of thin leather, 3 ins x ¼ in, to the shaft to form a ¼ in. loop at the end.

C

Now bind with thread two of the 'fluffies' to the front and two to the back of the feather as shown. Or you can wrap both loop and fluffies with a strip of adhesive tape. The fluffies fill the gap between the binding and the vanes and should form a thick ruff above the red binding.

D

Then wrap with a piece of 2¼ ins. red felt or flannel and cement at the back. Finally bind with yarn or very thin string – white or yellow, if possible.

A

B

C

ADHESIVE
TAPE CAN BE
USED FOR
BINDING

THE COMPLETED
FEATHER SHOULD LOOK
LIKE THIS. GLUE A TINY
CHICKEN FLUFFY TO THE TIP

HOW TO MAKE..........
An Indian War Bonnet continued

The skull cap should be made from the crown of an old felt hat. Draw a chalk line round 1 in. above the base at the front and ½ in. at the back. Start at the centre front and cut two slits ¼ in. deep and ¼ in. apart. Cut these in pairs all round the hat as shown leaving ⅜ in. between each pair.

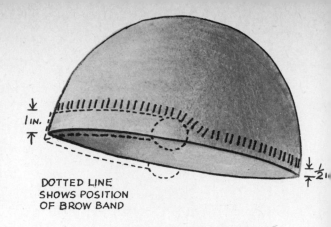

DOTTED LINE
SHOWS POSITION
OF BROW BAND

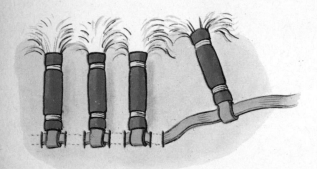

There are left and right curved feathers. Divide accordingly, choose the straightest for the front, and start lacing from the centre and work both ways to the back. The illustration shows how the lacing is taken through the loops and the slits in the hat. Tie lace at the back.

Now you are ready to give the bonnet its shape. With a fine awl bore a hole through each feather 5ins. above the lacing loop. Take care not to break the quill. Then, with a needle and thread sew carefully through each quill and adjust them to shape the bonnet to the right flare. A touch of cement will hold the feathers in place. Tie thread at back.

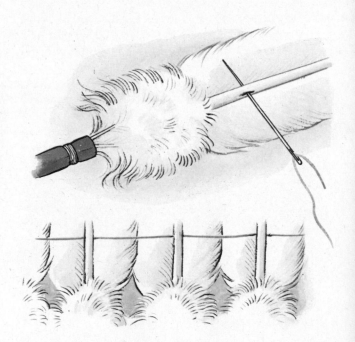

GLUE FLUFFIES ALL OVER CROWN

FASTEN PLUME HERE

Having got a good shape to the bonnet, the finishing touches can now be done. Make a brow-band either by beadwork on canvas, or by painting. Reinforce the canvas then sew to the hat in the position indicated above. Make and attach side roundels in a similar way. The side drops are lengths of white rabbit fur with dark fur glued to the end. Finally, attach a stripped feather to the crown as shown, then cover the crown with small fluffies.

THE CEREMONIAL 'WAR SHIRT'

The buckskin war shirt was worn by important men on ceremonial occasions. Make yours from unbleached calico, or similar cloth, dyed a pale fawn. Using an old shirt as a guide, cut a paper pattern. Make it full and roomy. Sew back and front together at the shoulders and hem all edges except the bottom which should have a 3 in. fringe. Cut sleeves as shown and sew to shoulders, leaving sides open. Both sleeves and sides of shirt are tied together at intervals with thongs or tapes. The neck opening should be wide enough to slip over the head.

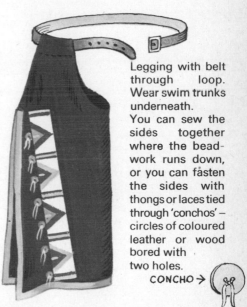

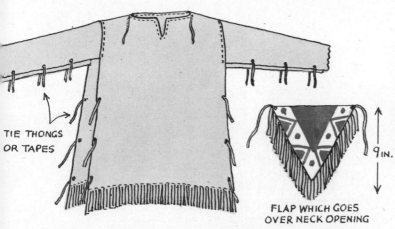

TIE THONGS OR TAPES

FLAP WHICH GOES OVER NECK OPENING

9 IN.

The triangular neck piece can be made from cloth or coloured felt with wash leather fringe, and decorated with either beadwork or paint. It is tied with tapes to cover the neck opening and comes tight to the neck. The strips of beadwork can be imitated by painting white canvas with Indian designs and sewing the strips on to the shirt. They are 3 ins. wide and the lengths that go over the shoulders are from 30 ins. to 36 ins. long.

The sleeves and sides of the shirt are not sewn together but are tied at intervals with thongs or tapes. The fitting is very loose.

LEGGINGS

Leggings are best made from heavy navy blue or red cloth. Measure yourself for a pattern then cut to the shape shown, hem the top edges and bind the sides and bottom with coloured tape. Fold the top over to make a loop for the belt. Don't forget to reverse for the opposite leg.

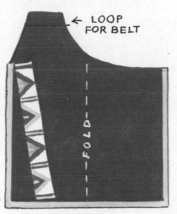

LOOP FOR BELT

WAIST HIGH

FOLD

INSIDE LEG

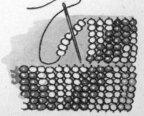

Legging with belt through loop. Wear swim trunks underneath.
You can sew the sides together where the beadwork runs down, or you can fasten the sides with thongs or laces tied through 'conchos' – circles of coloured leather or wood bored with two holes.

CONCHO →

KNIFE SHEATHS were made from rawhide covered by beaded buckskin. Make yours from leather with a fringe of chamois leather sewn on. Try beadwork if you can on a canvas cover or paint with Indian designs as shown.

LEATHER BELT LOOP

BEADWORK

Sew beads on to canvas using the Lazy Squaw stitch. Mark out your design and sew in the way shown in ½ in. wide strips. The strips run lengthways in all cases.

String 6 or 7 beads on the thread and catch at the end. Continue in this way to form strips.

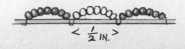

< ½ IN. >

Telephoning the Emergency Services

1

In an emergency, keep calm.

2

Find out how to get in touch by telephone with the Emergency Services in your area BEFORE an emergency. Dialling '999' is probably correct but this can depend on where you are and what telephone you use. A quick way to find out is to read the dial label of the telephone. Emergency call instructions are displayed in telephone kiosks.

3

Although a telephone in a kiosk may APPEAR to be 'out of order', you may still be able to make an emergency call. Lift the handset. If you hear 'dialling tone' (a continuous purring sound) you should be able to make your call.

4

After dialling, when the Post Office operator answers, LISTEN CAREFULLY to what she asks. Tell her what emergency service you require. (If you do not know which Emergency Service you need, or if you require more than one, ask for 'Police'). She will want to know the number of the telephone YOU are using. Give her the number clearly and accurately.

5

When she has connected you to the Emergency Service, do LISTEN CAREFULLY to the person speaking to you. He will ask what the trouble is, where it is, and from where you are telephoning. Answer clearly and correctly.

6

When you have finished the call, remember to replace the handset on the telephone rest.

7

This is how to dial '999' in the dark

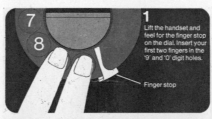

1 Lift the handset and feel for the finger stop on the dial. Insert your first two fingers in the '9' and '0' digit holes.

Finger stop

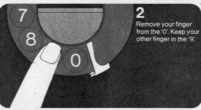

2 Remove your finger from the '0'. Keep your other finger in the '9'.

3 Dial right round to the finger stop.

4 Take finger out. Let the dial return freely.

Dial '9' in this way three times.

If you wish to telephone an Emergency Service on a matter which is not urgent, you must ring on its ordinary number. You will find this in the telephone directory.

Fire

Air/Sea

Ambulance

Post Office Telecommunications

REPRODUCED BY KIND PERMISSION OF THE POST OFFICE

Remember emergency calls are free of charge.

Police

A Post Office telephone operator at an emergency position in an exchange

Cave/Mountain Rescue

Coastguard

INSIDE A LIGHTHOUSE

by Peter Stuckey

This illustration shows a typical rock lighthouse. Some, like Bishop Rock, now have a helicopter platform.

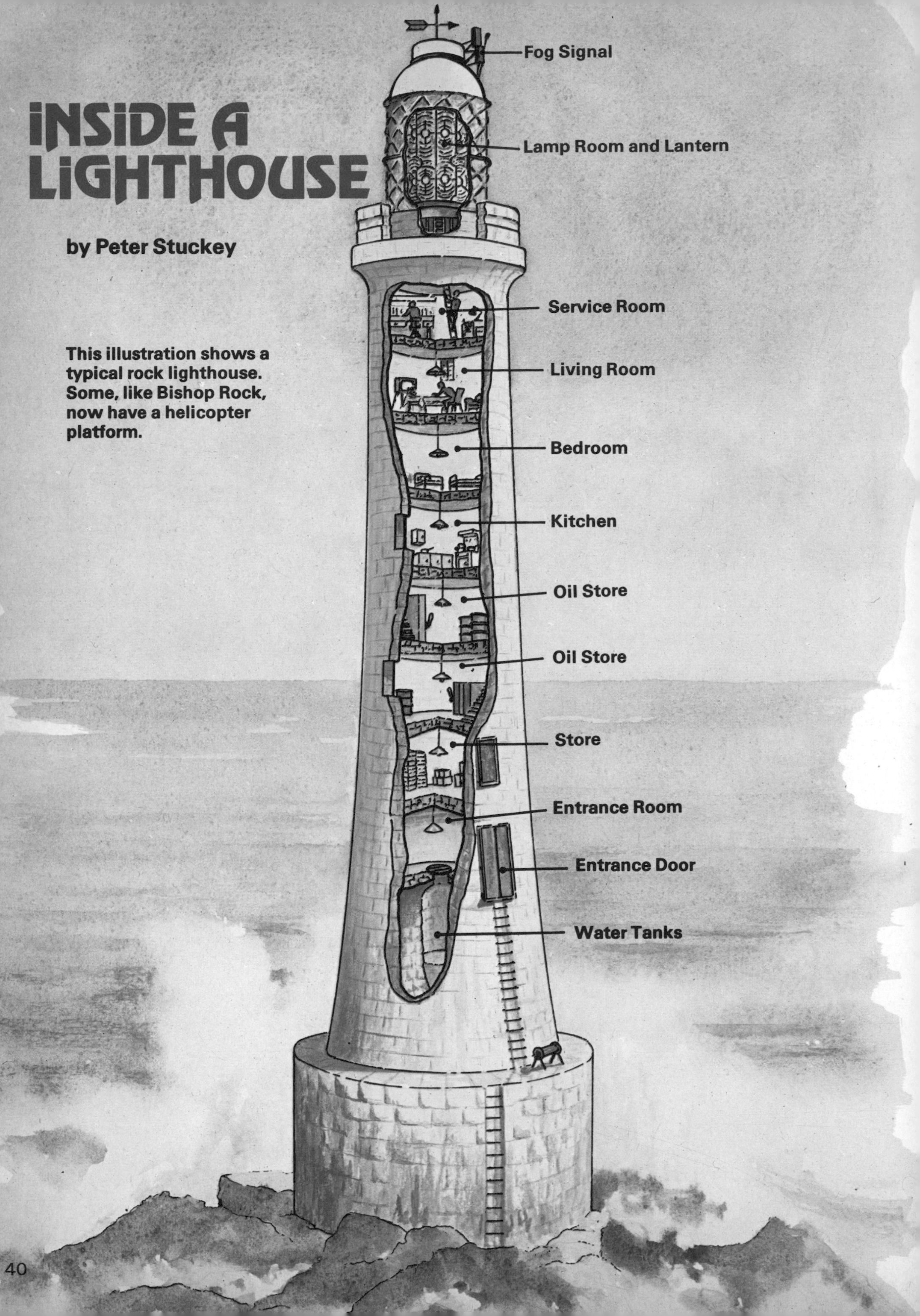

Fog Signal

Lamp Room and Lantern

Service Room

Living Room

Bedroom

Kitchen

Oil Store

Oil Store

Store

Entrance Room

Entrance Door

Water Tanks

Focus on TRINITY HOUSE

The Master, Wardens and Assistants of the Guild, Fraternity or Brotherhood of the Most Glorious Undivided Trinity and of St. Clement in the Parish of Deptford Strond in the County of Kent, commonly known as The Corporation of Trinity House. And what's Trinity House, you may ask?

The Corporation was originally a Guild of Mariners or Pilots, but today the members of the Corporation as such do not pilot ships but among their other duties they issue licences to nearly 650 Pilots whom they have examined and who are eligible to pilot ships in and out of British ports. Members of the Trinity House Board in their vessel PATRICIA have the privilege to escort the Sovereign when the Royal Yacht is entering or leaving Pilotage Waters.

Over the years Trinity House has assumed other functions and the one for which it is best known is the operation of lighthouses in England and Wales. The association between Trinity House and seamarks arose from an Act of Parliament in the reign of Queen Elizabeth I, which gave it the right to set up "such and so many beacons, marks and signs for the sea in such place or places of the sea-shores and uplands near the sea-coasts". The question of whether lighthouses came under the terms of this Act was disputed for a long time and it wasn't until 1836 that Parliament decided to give to Trinity House the powers to buy out those lighthouses which were privately owned.

The first lighthouse to be built in England was the Pharos at Dover when the Romans came across the Channel. The remains of this can still be seen today high on the cliffs overlooking the Strait. The first of the modern lighthouses to be built was at Lowestoft in Suffolk in 1609. Today, there are 92 lighthouses under the jurisdiction of Trinity House, some on land and some out at sea; some that are manned and some that are automatic. A shore station is one that is actually on the mainland and the Keepers live with their families in houses nearby. The type of lighthouse which is out at sea is called a rock station. For each 'rock' there are three Keepers on duty for one month at a time. They then spend one month ashore on holiday.

Just imagine for a moment that you are a Keeper at a rock station like Bishop Rock off Lands End. You've had your month's leave and you are in a helicopter heading out towards your second home for another spell of duty. Keepers are flown to and from their places of duty by the helicopter operated by Trinity House and it lands on a specially built platform. The sea is choppy, but not too rough. You are approaching the tower that rises 167 feet out of the water, with the waves slapping against its sides. It looks like a model as you look down on it, but you know that it is built on firm foundations – interlocking granite blocks, which are 41 feet in diameter at the bottom and 23 feet at high water mark. You land quickly on the pad and exchange a few words with the mate whom you are relieving, and off he goes in the helicopter that within a few minutes will deliver him maybe to within sight of his home. And you enter the tower, your second home which isn't a bit like the home you left ashore.

What are the duties of a Lighthouse Keeper? At night the light has to be attended and watched without a break and the fog signal has to be sounded at times of poor visibility. During the day the lighthouse apparatus with its 350 square feet of glass has to be polished and maintained at peak efficiency. Then there are all the domestic duties, for the Keepers on these rock stations can't take their wives with them!

There are several other ways in which Trinity House helps ships to keep on their right courses. Some twenty-one Lightvessels are moored at strategic points to mark hazards in the sea. These ships which have no engines with which to propel themselves cannot seek shelter in the storms but must remain on station to warn other ships of peril. In recent years some Lightvessels have been replaced by Large Automatic Navigation Buoys (LANBY). These can stay on station for six months without servicing. Also serving as aids to navigation are about 600 buoys, two thirds of which are lit. These complete the way in which Trinity House serves the mariner and ensures that ships of all nations are amply supplied with the signposts of the sea to enable them to go their way in safety.

Last, but by no means least, Trinity House maintains a home at Walmer in Kent for retired Master Mariners who need a safe harbour after braving storms over many years.

THE CUB SCOUT ANNUAL acknowledges the co-operation of Trinity House in the preparation of this article.

In quest of EXCALIBUR

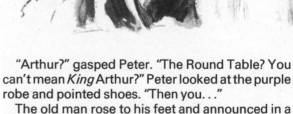

By Tilly Wingrave

The mist swirled over the surface of the lake, thinning as the autumn sunshine began to break through. Peter was about to throw a stick into the water when he stopped and stared as a punt glided into view. It wasn't so much the sight of the punt that surprised him, as the tall figure of an elderly gentleman who clung, somewhat inexpertly, to the quant and wore what appeared to be a long, purple dressing-gown.

Then Peter noticed that the punt was sinking lower and lower until it disappeared slowly out of sight below the surface of the water. The old man hitched up his robe, waded through the shallow water, scrambled up the bank and sat down on a fallen tree. He began to take off his shoes which, to Peter's amazement, had long, curling points at the toes.

The old man emptied the water out of his shoes, tied the toes together and hung them on a branch to dry. The knot began to slip . . . and slip . . . until *flup!* The shoes fell to the ground.

With a sigh, the old man picked them up and re-tied the knot.

"That's still a granny," said Peter.

"What?" exclaimed the old man, noticing Peter for the first time. "What did you say?"

"That's a granny knot," repeated Peter. "It'll come undone again. Let me show you." Taking the shoes, he tied the toes together with a reef knot.

"Very nice! Where did you learn to do that?"

"At Cubs," replied Peter.

"At *whats?*" exclaimed the man.

Briefly Peter told the gentleman about Scouting.

The stranger's face cleared. "Ah, I understand," he nodded. "These 'Scouts' are knights, and the 'Cubs' are their squires!"

"Well, not exactly," began Peter. But the man wasn't listening.

"It seems little has changed since my day," he commented. "But I doubt whether any Scouts are finer knights than those who sat with Arthur and me at the Round Table!"

"Arthur?" gasped Peter. "The Round Table? You can't mean *King* Arthur?" Peter looked at the purple robe and pointed shoes. "Then you. . ."

The old man rose to his feet and announced in a strong voice: "I am MERLIN!"

"But what are you doing here?" asked Peter.

Merlin sat down again. "It's all King Arthur's doing," he replied glumly. "I told him it was a waste of a perfectly good sword when he threw Excalibur into the lake . . ."

"Well?" prompted Peter, after Merlin had lapsed into a gloomy silence.

"Now he wants it back!" Merlin wriggled his toes up and down. "He's sent me to fetch it. It's in this lake. But how can I possibly find it, let alone get it out?"

Peter pushed his hands deep into his pockets, as he always did when he was thinking. His fingers felt the cool, polished case of his compass.

"I've got it!" Peter exclaimed suddenly. "We can use my compass!"

over one side, holding the compass over the water.

"Stop!" cried Peter suddenly, "The needle's moved!" The raft slid slowly on. "Now it's turning the other way. We must have passed right over something made of iron!" Peter grasped the boathook and groped in the murky water. "I've got something! It's heavy!"

Merlin steadied the raft as Peter struggled and heaved. At last something appeared.

"A rusty bicycle frame!" Peter sighed. Merlin wanted to ask Peter what it was, but the boy had already let it go and said, "Let's try again."

One dented bucket, two pram wheels and a battered saucepan later, Merlin and Peter sat despondently on the bank.

"I'm sorry that didn't work," said Peter apologetically. He thought for a moment. "Perhaps someone has already found Excalibur!" he suggested.

"If any man had, you would have heard of it," Merlin assured him, "for he would be the finest swordsman in the land."

"We don't use swords any more," Peter remarked. "Something like Excalibur would be in a museum now."

"Museum? What's that?" Merlin asked.

"A place where old or interesting things are kept, so that people can go and look at them. Come to think of it," Peter went on, "there's a museum in town. Perhaps it's there. Let's go and look."

Merlin pulled on his shoes, which were dry now. "Young people haven't changed," he mumbled, as he followed in Peter's footsteps. "Always in a hurry!"

They reached the entrance to the museum. Fortunately there were few people about and those that were didn't really give Merlin a second glance, thinking he was a hippie or something like that.

Peter led the way through the doors into the museum. Merlin stopped in his tracks.

"Surely this must be the home of some great magician," he whispered. "Look how these beasts are frozen in mid-stride!"

"It's not magic," Peter assured him. "They're stuffed. Hey, what are you doing?"

"Never fear!" cried Merlin. He took a pouch of grey powder from his pocket and sprinkled a handful over Peter. "This will protect you from the wizard's spells."

"But . . . ah-CHOO! . . . I tell you . . . ah-TISH-OO! There is no wizard," sneezed Peter. He took out his handkerchief and wiped the powder from his streaming eyes, then looked round.

Merlin had disappeared.

Peter hurried from the room, and into the corridor beyond. There was still no sign of Merlin. However, on the wall opposite was a sign which read 'HISTORICAL COSTUMES: ARMOURY'.

"What's that?" asked Merlin.

Peter showed him.

"Ah, yes!" replied Merlin. "The loadstone! But how will this help us to find Excalibur?"

"The needle usually points to north," explained Peter. "But when it comes near iron it points to that instead. We'll hold the compass over the water, then if we pass near the sword the needle will point to it."

"But how can we? My punt's sunk," Merlin said.

"We built a raft at Cubs last week," Peter said. "It's hidden over there in the reeds. Come on." They got up and as Peter led the way to the reed bed, he added: "We made it from an old table-top, with some blown up plastic sacks fastened round the sides. It's got a piece of wood for a paddle, and there's an old boat-hook too. We can use that to fish up the sword if we find it. The water isn't very deep."

A few minutes later the raft was gliding across the lake, with Merlin paddling and Peter leaning

Illustrated by Glenn Rix

"Armoury! That's where he'll be," murmured Peter to himself.

Passing through the Historical Costumes section, he came across one of the museum attendants muttering darkly to himself as he brushed some of Merlin's grey powder from the figure of a lady in 6th century costume.

"What happened?" asked Peter.

"Be careful," the attendant replied. "There's a looney in a dressing gown wandering about. I found him trying to talk to this figure. When I spoke to him he stared at me as if I was some kind of monster, then he threw all this dust in the air, and ran away."

"Which way did he go?" asked Peter.

The attendant nodded towards the door which led to the Armoury.

As Peter hurried into the Armoury, he saw his favourite exhibit. Against a painted background of a battle scene two suits of armour had been arranged to look like two knights in hand-to-hand combat. One held his shield high to ward off a blow from the other's upraised sword. Peter stopped suddenly. The knight's hand was empty! Where was the sword?

"Merlin!" groaned Peter. But surely that battered old sword couldn't be Excalibur?

Peter looked all round the room. Where had the old magician gone? A sound from a door at the far end of the room attracted his attention and he saw Merlin walking rather awkwardly towards the exit.

"Wait for me!" Peter exclaimed, running to catch up to the magician.

"Eh?" Merlin gave a start. With a clatter a heavy sword fell from beneath his robe.

Peter picked it up. "Is *this* Excalibur?" he asked.

"Well, no!" admitted Merlin. "But Arthur's memory isn't what it used to be. I'm sure he won't know the difference."

"But you can't take it," protested Peter. "It belongs to the museum."

Merlin stiffened at the sound of approaching footsteps. "The magician!" he whispered. "He came upon me back yonder, as I was trying to free a maiden from his spell. But I fear his magic was too strong for me!"

"That's not a magician!" Peter assured him. "It's one of the museum attendants, and it wasn't a maiden, just a wax dummy, to show how people used to dress. Still," he went on, "he mustn't find us with the sword." He hid the sword in a tall Chinese vase. "Come on, we'd better go before you get into *real* trouble." Taking Merlin's arm he steered him firmly through the exit, down the road and towards the lake.

"What will Arthur say when you go back without Excalibur?" asked Peter, when they were back at the water's edge.

"I won't be able to go back at all without my boat," Merlin pointed out sadly.

"You can take the Cubs' raft," said Peter. "I'm sure the others will understand when I tell them why you needed it."

"Thank you," answered Merlin. "And never fear, your raft will be back in its place tomorrow morning."

"But how?" asked Peter.

Merlin smiled mysteriously. "I still have some powers," he replied, "even if the great Wizard Museum was too strong for me." He looked across the water. "I must be on my way now. The mist is getting thick again."

Peter helped Merlin onto the raft and pushed it away from the shore. Merlin paddled further and further out. Suddenly Peter's eyes almost popped out of his head. At the edge of the curtain of swirling mist the water became agitated. A white-draped arm, clasping a gleaming sword, rose slowly from the water. Three times it flourished the sword, then as Merlin leant towards it with an outstretched hand, the mist closed down, blotting the scene from view.

But Peter was left with the strong feeling that Merlin's quest for Excalibur had, in the end, been successfully completed.

CROSSWORD All About Music

by Daphne Pilcher

Clue Across:

3. The notes F, A, C, E, are written in these (6)
8. Soup - an anagram of a word describing a musical composition (4)
9. Musical term for very slowly (5)
10. Another term for a round (5)
12. When everyone sings together it is called singing in − − − − − − (6)
14. Signs showing that the notes following must be played a semi-tone higher (6)
18. In singing, the name given to the highest pitch of male voice (4)
20. On the drums (4)
21. Play set to music (5)
22. This can be tolled or rung (4)
23. Harp not now in use (4)
24. Story danced in mime (6)
26. Piece of music with several movements (6)
31. Sad, rather slow rag-time song of Negro origin (5)
32. French composer who wrote *Bolero* (5)
33. One of the thin raised pieces of metal running across the neck of stringed instrument (4)
34. Keyboard of organ operated by the feet (6)

Clues Down:

1. Violins are played with these (4)
2. Groups of movements (6)
4. Chime of bells (4)
5. Refrain (6)
6. Instrument played by American negroes (5)
7. Country dancing (4)
11. Tenor violin (5)
13. Composer of *La Traviata* (5)
15. Home of the Promenade Concerts: The Royal Albert − − − − (4)
16. Could be a bag, might be a reed, instrument (4)
17. Bass violin (5)
18. Solo song in an opera or cantata (4)
19. Woodwind instrument (4)
21. Usually played in church (5)
24. A simple, sentimental song (6)
25. Male voices between altos and basses (6)
27. Piece for eight performers (5)
28. Another name for several of 18 down (4)
29. Lively Scottish dance (4)
30. A stringed instrument popular from 14th to 17th century (4)

Solution on page 63

Don't eat that coconut –
There might be a Hermit inside!

by Geoffrey Hemming
illustrated by Glenn Rix

If you ever visit a tropical country on your holidays don't rush up to the first coconut you find on the beach with the hope of eating it. You could have quite a shock if you do, for that coconut may well be the home of a hermit crab!

Hermit crabs can be found anywhere in the world and they don't all live in the sea! Some make their homes on land and they've even been found living in trees.

The ones that settle in water prefer places that have a sandy or muddy bottom, while the tropical species move into the stems of plants, bamboo shoots and coconut shells.

The Hermit crab is rightly named because, just like real hermits, they like to hide themselves away. They can often be found hiding in shells that had once belonged to other types of sea creatures.

The female Hermit crab lays her eggs and then carries them around with her until they hatch out. Immediately the baby crabs seek out a shell to live in to protect them from the dangers of the sea. Many are caught and eaten by larger predators before they have the chance to reach safety. Those that find themselves a shell live in it until they grow so big it no longer fits them. Then they move out and hunt for a larger shell.

In the world there are approximately 4,500 different species of crabs and they have all sorts of odd names. To name but a few, there are Spider crabs; King crabs; Mole crabs; Robber crabs; Fiddler crabs; Pea crabs; Lantern crabs and perhaps the one I like best, Ghost crabs.

The most frightening in appearance could well be the Robber crab for they grow to an enormous size and can weigh anything up to 37 pounds!

Their main diet is coconuts and they chip open the shells with their huge pincers to get at the contents. The female Robber crab lays her young in the sea and after birth they immediately hatch into zoeæ, which is the first larval stage. After 20 to 30 days the zoeæ change into glaucothoe, the intermediate stage. They then leave the sea to live in sea shells and stay in them for about 3 to 4 weeks.

After this the young crabs discard their protective shells and bury themselves in moist sand where they develop into their final adult stage. During daylight Robber crabs stay buried about 2 feet under the sand and only emerge at night to seek food.

So, if you ever find a coconut on a beach and decide to eat it check inside first to see it isn't housing a hermit – otherwise you might be the one who gets bitten!

Eric Franklin tells you how to make

An emergency CUP

By using kitchen foil you can make a cup which folds flat and can be slipped into any pocket, yet be ready when you need it. You can even make several so that there is one for each of your friends.

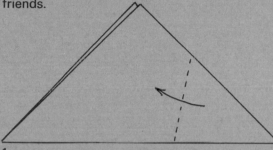

1.
Foil is quite fragile, so always try to use it doubled. Cut a piece of foil 20 x 40 cms (8 inches by 16 inches) and fold it in half, making a square with 20 cms (8 inch) sides. Treat as a single sheet of paper and fold in half diagonally. Fold one of the bottom corners to the opposite side as shown by the dotted line.

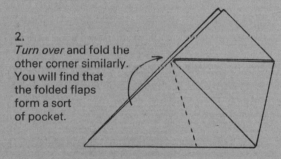

2.
Turn over and fold the other corner similarly. You will find that the folded flaps form a sort of pocket.

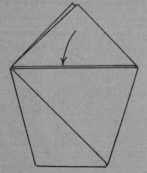

3. & 4.
Fold the top corners down into the pockets, one on each side and your cup is complete.

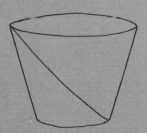

In an emergency you can make this cup from a piece of stout paper (not newspaper) and it will actually hold water long enough to give you a drink.

ABOUT THE 'SAVE IT' GAME ON PAGE 34

This game takes the players into all kinds of houses — old houses, new houses, country houses, town houses, cottages and bungalows. The families who live in these homes all use some kind of fuel to give them heat and hot water and to cook their food. In some of the houses fuel is used carefully and in others it is wasted.

These notes give you the reasons why you can go forward on some squares and back on others. The numbers are those of the squares.

SQUARES

3 (go forward to 14)	The warmth from inside a house escapes in many ways but most would escape through the roof if the roof space were not 'insulated'. Roof insulation is being laid in this picture.
7 (miss one go)	The heat should have been turned off as soon as the kettle boiled.
10 (go forward to 22)	Turning down the 'thermostat' to a heating system by even one degree will save fuel and money.
15 (take one extra go)	This is a hot water cylinder being fitted with a thick jacket to keep the heat in.
18 (go back to 8)	He is too hot so why not turn off the radiator?
23 (move forward to 38)	This housewife has planned her meal so that she can make full use of her oven, and not heat it up for just one dish.
27 (take two extra goes)	Taking a shower instead of a bath can save a lot of hot water — and therefore a lot of fuel.
31 (move forward to 40)	This is what Number 18 should have done.
37 (go back to 21)	Every time a television is switched on, more fuel is needed at the power station. It is a waste of fuel to leave a television on when no one is watching it.
43 (go back to 26)	The flames should be underneath the pan, not around the sides.
50 (go back to 42)	About a quarter of all the fuel used in the average home is used for heating water. Fuel is therefore wasted when a hot water tap is left to drip.
61 (miss one go)	Keep doors and windows shut to keep in the heat.
66 (go back to 52)	The owner of this house should take a tip from Number 15.

SOLUTION ON PAGE 63

THE TRICKY TRAIL

SOME STALWART LADS FOUND THEMSELVES IN THE MIDDLE OF A DARK WOOD THAT WAS FULL OF UNSEEN HAZARDS. IT WAS VERY EASY TO GET SWALLOWED UP IN MARSHY GROUND AND THINGS TOO TERRIBLE TO MENTION. THEY HAD A MAP MARKING ALL THE TREES AND A VITAL INSTRUCTION TELLING THEM HOW TO GET OUT SAFELY— "YOU MUST MOVE FROM TREE TO TREE IN THE ORDER 1-4 AND YOU MUST ONLY MOVE VERTICALLY AND HORIZONTALLY —NOT DIAGONALLY"

1 2 3 4

CAN YOU GET OUT OF THE WOOD?

Be an URBAN NATURALIST

Some people think that you can only be a naturalist if you live right out in the country, but that just is not true! Animals, birds, insects and wild plants can all be found in towns, perhaps not in the really busy streets, but certainly in parks and back gardens, on empty building sites, on playing fields, sewage farms, along the banks of canals and on road verges and along footpaths.

I have seen a wild duck nesting beside a little pond on the roof garden of a big London store, and pigeons certainly prefer town life to country living. During the winter thousands of starlings come into our big cities at night to roost on the ledges of buildings, kestrels make their nests on high towers, and owls settle in old trees in the parks. Many smaller birds – like sparrows, tits and chaffinches – can be found in town gardens, and lakes in the parks always attract mallards and other ducks.

Some years ago I noticed a sparrow's nest which was built in a drainpipe leading from the guttering of a town house. One day a very heavy rain storm washed the whole nest right down the pipe and drowned the hen who was sitting on the eggs. The cock sparrow searched for his mate everywhere, peering down the pipe and cheeping anxiously, hoping to get a reply. He stayed around for about ten days before moving away from his ruined home.

A friend of mine who lived in a Lancashire town noticed that the lid of his dustbin was being knocked off nearly every night, so he decided to keep watch one evening, and just as it was getting dark he saw a fox creep up and sniff at the bin. It rose on its hind legs, gave the lid a push with its nose and then started to pull out the rubbish, searching for something to eat. Next day my friend fixed up his camera at a window overlooking the back yard and took a photograph of the raider.

On the next pages you can see, and read about, some of the plants, animals and birds you should find in your home town.

By L. Hugh Newman

Illustrated by Peter Harrison

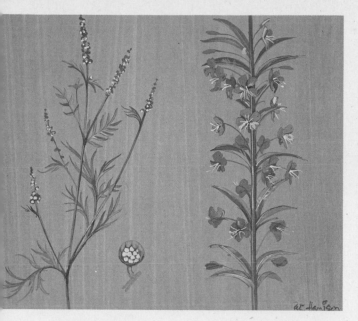

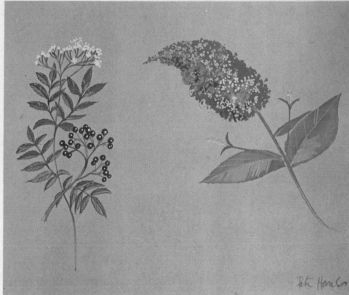

WORMWOOD AND WILLOWHERB

The wormwood, with its grey-green, finely divided leaves, which have a rather strong aromatic smell, and its small yellowish flowers, is a waste land weed that you often find in town alleys and on empty building sites.

The beautiful willowherb, or fireweed, is a plant which quickly appears on any empty town site, and it always grows along railway lines. When it is seeding, the fluffy, fly-away seeds get pulled along by the draught made by passing trains and so are carried right into the towns, where the wind helps to distribute them to many places where they can find a little soil or gravel to grow in.

THE ELDER AND THE BUDDLEIA

The elder bush can grow even from a crack in a wall and will spring up again from the root even if it is cut right down. Birds love the berries which ripen at the end of the summer and spread the seeds around in their droppings. That is why we find elders growing in all kinds of unlikely places, where their white flowers make a fine show in early summer.

The purple buddleia, which is really a garden shrub, also seeds itself in any open space, in abandoned gardens or on the walls of tumble-down houses and empty factories. When it is in bloom many butterflies visit the flowers.

BUTTERFLIES

The three butterflies which you are most likely to see in a town are the small tortoiseshell, the peacock and the red admiral. They all like to visit garden flowers in search of nectar. As they lay their eggs on stinging nettles which grow near houses and round allotments and playing fields, they can quite easily breed in a town year after year. The tortoiseshell and the peacock spend the winter hibernating in sheds and houses in dark corners, but the red admirals usually move away south in the autumn and a new generation arrives from France in the late spring.

HARVEST MICE

The little harvest mice are not really town animals, but you might see them in cornfields outside country towns. They are very agile and can climb grasses and corn stalks, clinging on, not only with their paws but with their tails as well. They are clever builders, too, and make their nests from woven grasses fixed between three or four corn stalks well above ground level. Here the tiny babies are born and reared and when they are big enough to leave the nest they can be seen scampering and playing together and rushing back to hide in the nest when they are frightened.

THE HEDGEHOG

The hedgehog is an animal that comes and goes as it pleases and it is quite at home in town gardens and parks. Unlike the rabbit, a hedgehog is a useful animal to have around because it eats slugs and snails, beetles and caterpillars. It is also very fond of bread and milk and if you see one in your garden and then put out a saucer of this food every evening you will soon find that it becomes quite tame and expects to be fed regularly. During the winter hedgehogs like to curl up and sleep in drifts of old leaves and dead grass in a quiet corner.

THE FOX

This picture, which shows a fox visiting a dustbin, tells you that it is quite a large animal and not unlike a dog in appearance. Foxes are real scavengers and not at all afraid of walking around in towns during the night when the streets are quiet and empty. Many of them have their homes, which are called 'earths' on the railway banks just outside the town and will come running in along the line at night. Sometimes one can hear them barking to each other, or to the female foxes (which are called vixens), howling in an eerie kind of way.

THE BLACK REDSTART

This very smart-looking little bird nested for the first time in England in 1923 and since then it has slowly increased in numbers year by year. Originally the birds made their nests on cliffs by the sea, but then they began to appear in towns. After the Second World War in 1945 several pairs nested among the ruins in the City of London. Now they are found in several towns on the east coast, as far north as Norfolk, and right round into Sussex. The atomic power station at Dungeness in Kent is one of the places where this bird has settled.

THE BARN OWL

The ghostly-looking barn owl seldom visits large cities, but in smaller country towns it is not unusual to see these birds flying round at dusk, hunting for mice and rats. Barn owls like to nest with a roof over their heads, and church towers and the attics of old houses are very much to their liking. All they ask is that a window should be left permanently open so that they can fly in and out unhindered. They are very useful birds and destroy large numbers of field mice and voles.

THE SONG THRUSH

The song thrush has long since adapted itself to a life side by side with people. It likes to be in gardens, where it can make its nest in some thick hedge and pick up worms from the lawn and in the vegetable garden when the soil is being cultivated. One of its favourite foods is garden snails and every thrush finds a stone or brick or even an old bottle on which it can smash the snail shells. This place is known as the thrush's anvil and if you see a lot of broken snail shells in one place and then watch from a distance, you will almost certainly see the thrush coming there again to break the next snail it finds.

THE HERON

Although the grey heron is in many ways a shy bird and would never nest in a town, it is not afraid of coming close to houses in the early morning, when most people are still asleep and it has a good chance of catching a fine lot of goldfish in various garden ponds. It will visit lakes in the parks as well, or fish from a river bank right in the middle of a town, standing as still as a statue until it sees a fish within reach. It then plunges its long sharp beak into the water to capture it. Many people cover their garden ponds with netting so that herons cannot get the fish.

THE SEAGULL

If you live in a town which is near the sea, or on a river, you will have seen the seagulls many times down by the harbour or along the sea front and on the beach. They also come and settle on playing fields and in parks and big gardens. The rubbish dumps outside the town are often swarming with squabbling gulls and if there is a market place in the town they are sure to come in to see what they can pick up when the stalls are taken down. In many places gulls also nest on the roofs of houses or on the window ledges of factory buildings.

This magnificent map shows a wide variety of native British wildlife found throughout England, Scotland and Wales. It has been reproduced from a poster by kind permission of The Society for the Promotion of Nature Conservation.

The Society, which was granted a new Royal Charter in 1976 to promote nature conservation, particularly in Britain, is the national association of the 41 Nature Conservation Trusts which cover England and Wales, mainly on a county basis, Scotland and Northern Ireland.

The SPNC and the Trusts have established over 1000 nature reserves where the conservation of wildlife is the first priority. But they are equally concerned with taking practical steps to conserve wild plants and animals in the countryside generally, through advice to landowners, through education and the promotion of a better understanding of nature amongst the public.

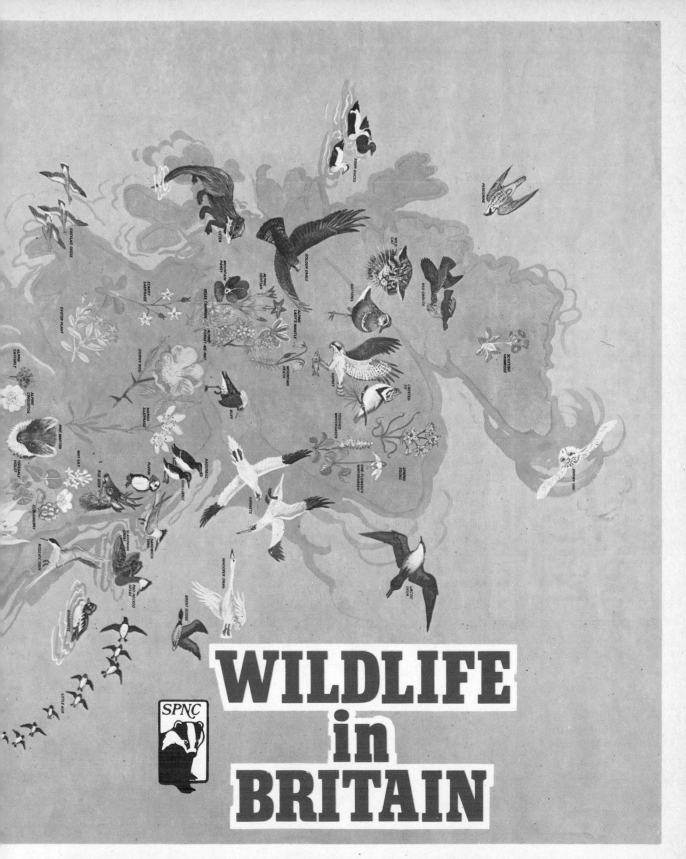

WILDLIFE in BRITAIN

Membership of the Trusts offers everyone the opportunity to support and participate in nature conservation in their own area according to their own skills and interests. The junior arm of the Trusts is the lively WATCH Environment Club (for young people aged 7-15 years old) with its own magazine *Watchword* which contains details of national projects and activities as well as news.

You can get membership forms and subscription details for the Trusts and the WATCH Environment Club by sending a stamped, self-addressed envelope to:

The Society for the Promotion of Nature Conservation, The Green, Nettleham, Lincoln, LN2 2NR.

The six High Speed Cub Scouts beside 'their' 125 train on Darlington Station.

Part 2

The Journey of a Lifetime

Words by David Harwood
Photographs by David Stower
(British Transport Films)

The time . . . 11.00 a.m. The date . . . Thursday 13th July 1978. The place . . . King's Cross Station, London. For Cub Scouts Russell Dale and Richard Neil of the Whiteleaf Pack, Princes Risborough, Buckinghamshire, it was the day when they would experience the journey of a lifetime. They were the guests of British Rail to find out what it was like to travel on the High Speed Train on behalf of *The Cub Scout Annual*.

Before the sleek, streamlined Inter-City 125 left London at 11.35 the boys were met by John Hughes (British Rail's Eastern Region Public Relations Officer) who took them to look inside the driver's cab and to meet the drivers — Douglas Hutchison and Jim Donaldson. Then Donald MacFadyen (British Rail's Circuit Group Manager at Newcastle-upon-Tyne), who had come down especially to see that the boys were given V.I.P. treatment, led them aboard through the extra wide entrance doors. The lads were at first startled, and then fascinated, by the sliding doors between the vestibule and the saloon which opened automatically when they walked on the tread mat.

"It's like being in the lounge at home," one of them remarked as he walked on the fitted carpet.

As the train slid smoothly and virtually silently out of the station, the boys settled down in their comfortable, colourful seats. They were travelling First Class, but were not in the least overwhelmed by their luxurious surroundings. Anyway, there was a lot to see both inside and outside the coach. Russell discovered that his seat was individually adjustable — and Richard was quick to follow suit!

They noticed that none of the windows opened. "That's because the whole train is air conditioned,"

Before the train leaves King's Cross Russell and Richard chat to the drivers.

explained John Fogg, who had co-ordinated the whole day for British Rail. "The windows are double glazed to reduce the noise, and they're tinted to stop undue glare from the sun."

And the sun *was* shining. It was a glorious day, just like the one when the Cub Scouts had visited Crewe six weeks before — and there hadn't been many decent days in between.

Fifteen minutes out of London, Chief Steward Arthur Kindlan invited the boys to take their seats in the restaurant car for lunch. They had hardly sat down before a voice over the public address system announced: "Ladies and gentlemen, you may be interested to know that we are now travelling at 125 miles an hour." Richard looked at Russell in disbelief. It just did not seem possible! They were eating in one of the fastest restaurants on earth!

The boys' faces tell their own story when Eric Donnison asks them if they would like to see his part of the train.

Russell tries out the telephone through which the guard speaks to the passengers over the public address system.

and so on. He showed them his two telephones – one for him to speak direct to the driver, the other through which he could speak to all the passengers over the public address system.

"Would you like to see the driver's cab at the back?" Mr. Donnison asked when the train stopped due to a temporary signal failure. Russell and Richard walked past the luggage van, and along the gangway through three doors into the rear driving cab. The tracks stretched out behind and as the boys sat in the two drivers' seats, clearance was given for the train to proceed. Of course, being in the 'back' power unit, the driving controls were inoperable.

Within a few minutes Doncaster's huge locomotive sheds slipped by and we stopped at Doncaster station, 156 miles out of London. Although 'visual' signals are not usually necessary to tell the driver of a 125 that he's clear to proceed (the telephone and an electronic 'bleep' are used), Mr. Donnison gave Russell his green flag to wave from the platform. The train gathered speed, and

Among the items of equipment Mr. Donnison shows the boys is his lamp with clear, red and green filters.

Both boys tucked into a magnificent meal, taking time between mouthfuls to look at the constantly changing scenery through the windows.

Huntingdon . . . Peterborough . . . Grantham . . .

During lunch the guard, Eric Donnison, introduced himself to the boys. "When you've finished, perhaps you'd like to come and see my part of the train."

"Yes, please!" the Cubs replied in unison, and the speed with which they ate noticeably increased. Mr. Donnison went about his duties up the train, but on his way back a little later, he stopped and gave each boy a small metal badge – the British Rail insignia from his uniform jacket.

"Would you like these as a little extra souvenir?" he asked with a smile. The expressions on the boys' faces, as well as their verbal "Thank yous" gave Mr. Donnison his answer.

A very special moment for Russell as he gives the 'go ahead' to leave Doncaster for York.

"Can we wear them on our uniforms . . . *please?*" Although 'officially' not part of the Cub Scout uniform, we felt sure that no one would mind, not on this special day!

Mr. Donnison took the boys back through the train. Several passengers looked very surprised – even envious – as Mr. Donnison unlocked the door and led the boys through into the power unit.

For the next half hour, Mr. Donnison showed the boys all his compartment's equipment, as well as revealing the 'secrets' of his brown leather case – lamps, flags,

the boys went back to their seats . . . but not for long!

The restaurant staff wanted to show the boys 'behind the scenes' of *their* part of the train. So into the kitchen they went with the chef, Mr. Gerry McGrady, who explained how such equipment as the microwave oven worked.

At York *we* had to move at high speed as we had arranged to meet Philip Barratt and Jonathan Garside of the 125th Derby Cub Scout Pack (who had been to Crewe with Russell and Richard six weeks before) and two local Cub Scouts – Paul Langstaff and Kevin Hollis of the Christ Church Pack, York. The Buckinghamshire boys ran up the platform to meet their brother Cub Scouts and everyone clambered aboard.

The boys meet the staff.

Chef Gerry McGrady reveals some of the secrets of his kitchen.

Up in the drivers' cab at 125 mph between York and Darlington. Note the ear muffs (left) which the boys wore on their way through the power unit.

The train gathered speed and headed north. With the co-operation of the drivers, Mr. Geoff Wilson (Motive Power Inspector at British Rail's York Headquarters) had arranged for the Cubs to go into *the* drivers' cab two at a time. Excitement mounted as Mr. Wilson gave the boys their instructions. The first pair put on ear muffs. By now the train was travelling at over 120 m.p.h. Passing the luggage compartment, Mr. Wilson opened the first door into the engine compartment. The wind rushed through the air vents at the side, tearing at their clothes and their hair. Even with the ear muffs, the noise of the engine was tremendous. Once through the second door it seemed much quieter and hotter as they walked beside the huge alternator to the third door which opened into the drivers' cab.

Drivers Douglas Hutchison and Jim Donaldson made the boys feel very much at home. The speedometer needle maintained a steady 120 – 125 m.p.h. Each time the train approached a signal, a bell rang. "If you look between the rails you'll see a short metal strip. If the line is clear and the signal green, the bell sounds. It means we can travel at speed even when visibility is poor."

Through the large windscreen the boys had a superb driver's eye view of the way ahead. It was so smooth and there was so little noise, that there was little sensation of speed unless you looked down at the blur of the concrete sleepers or noted the rapidity with which the

¼ mile posts flashed by beside the track . . . at 120 m.p.h. it takes only 30 seconds to cover a mile.

The sign marking the half way point between London and Edinburgh came and went in a trice, and it took just half an hour to eat up the 45 miles between York and Darlington. Darlington is the birthplace of railways in Britain and home of the first passenger locomotive – George Stephenson's Locomotion No. 1. We got out, and 'our' train continued its journey north. We waited for our High Speed Train back to York . . . for yet another surprise!

In the hot summer sunshine we walked from York Station to the National Railway Museum (which is part of the Science Museum, London) where Assistant Keeper Mr. P.W.B. Semmens was waiting to greet the Cubs. They could easily have spent hours looking round the two-acre Main Hall with its magnificent exhibits of locomotives and rolling stock spanning 150 years of railway history – what a terrific place for a Pack visit! – but our objective was to see the Experimental Advanced Passenger Train, in the compound just outside the main building. Mr. Semmens unlocked the door and let the boys climb up the steps into the driver's cab where they were confronted by ranks of push button controls, quite different from the High Speed Train.

Three pre-production Advanced Passenger Trains (APTs) are now undergoing extensive trials. It is hoped that the first production APT will come into service in 1979 between London and Glasgow . . . but that will be another story! It was time for the boys (and everyone else) to make tracks to their homes . . . in York, Derby, Princes Risborough, and elsewhere.

Russell and Richard looking round part of the National Railway Museum with the locomotives of years gone by.

The Cub Scouts inspecting the experimental Advanced Passenger Train at the National Railway Museum, York.

The CUB SCOUT ANNUAL thanks British Rail (Eastern Region) and many of their staff; the National Railway Museum (particularly Mr. P.W.B. Semmens); David Stower of British Transport Films, and the Cubs' Leaders without whose active co-operation this feature would not have been possible.

Try these ILLUSIONS and TEASERS!

Reproduced by courtesy of the Royal Society for the Prevention of Accidents

Study the two inside squares. Which would you say was the larger, the white square or the black one? Measure both with a ruler for the answer.

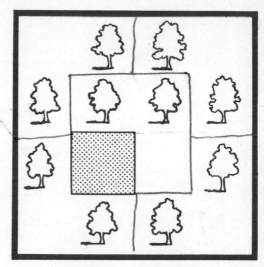

Divide the garden into five equal areas excluding the shaded area which represents the house. Each area must have straight borders and should contain two trees.

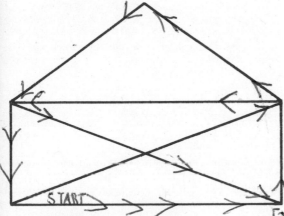

Can you draw this figure in one continuous line without raising the pencil from the paper?

FINISH

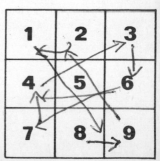

Arrange 11 matches into three squares as shown. Now make two squares by moving 3 matches only. Don't take any away.

Hold this diagram of circles at eye level and move the page in a circular motion. The circles will appear to rotate in the direction of the page movement.

Can you re-arrange the numbers in this diagram so that they always add up to 15 – across, downwards, or diagonally?

1	2	3
4	5	6
7	8	9

Answers on page 63.

Hallmarks on SILVER

HAVE YOU ever wondered what those funny little marks are on the backs of spoons or other silver things? Perhaps somebody has told you that an article is only real silver if there is a little lion stamped somewhere, which is certainly partly true. The little lion, however, isn't the only symbol stamped on the pieces — there will be several more.

These little stampings are known as Hall Marks and, to the expert, they tell the history of the piece of silver, the quality, where and when it was made and by whom it was made. They have been in existence for a very long time. Marks have occasionally been found on old Roman pieces of silver showing that even then there was some attempt at quality control, but the first legal control in England was made over 700 years ago. A law was introduced in 1238 AD followed by another in 1300AD which fixed the standard for silver as 'sterling', i.e. the same as for money, or rather the money of that period. It stated that 925 parts out of 1,000 must be pure silver. All silver of this standard was to be marked with a leopard's head and there were very heavy penalties if the stamp was misused, if for example, anyone cheated by putting the stamp on inferior silver. This law, or Ordinance as it was called, of 1300 AD lasted until 1856 — over 500 years — when certain modifications were made.

Another law, made in 1423 AD, confirmed the standard of silver and named seven towns to be set up as assay (testing) centres and each town adopted its own mark. Over the years these special centres have gradually changed and now there are only four — London, Birmingham, Sheffield and Edinburgh. Thus, the town in which the piece was first assayed will be known from the Town Mark. The current Town Marks are shown in the four drawings at the top of the next page, but it should be noted that before 1975 the mark for Sheffield silver was a crown.

by Eric Franklin

From early times each silversmith would put his own individual mark on his own work. At the beginning, initials were seldom used and the maker would use a symbol. For example, one well known Elizabethan maker stamped a sheep's head on his work while another used a key. Later, either the maker's initials or the first two letters of his surname were used. Here, then, is another mark, the maker's mark.

In 1544, Henry VIII debased the coinage: he reduced the amount of pure silver in coins, and people thought that the standards for silver wares would also become worse.

The Goldsmiths' Company, to reassure their patrons, introduced another mark to guarantee the standard of the silver, still 92.5%. This was the familiar lion, a lion *passant*. Such was the success of this mark that, even today over 400 years later, people will not believe a piece is truly silver unless they can see the lion. The lion, then is the third important mark.

From very early times in the marking of silver it became obligatory to include the date it was made. This was, and is, done by adding a

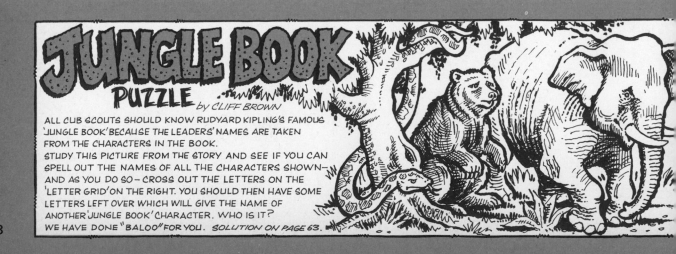

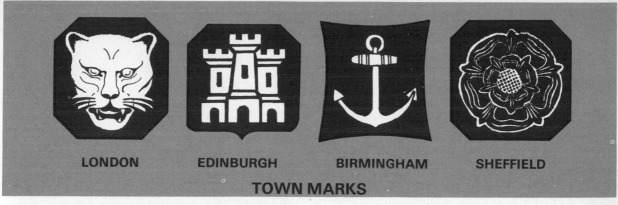

LONDON **EDINBURGH** **BIRMINGHAM** **SHEFFIELD**

TOWN MARKS

letter of the alphabet usually enclosed in a shield and a different letter (from A to V but omitting J) is used each year. By using different styles of letters and different shaped shields the possible combinations are almost endless so none have been, or will be, duplicated and the date can be fixed from this mark. Tables of all the date marks since the beginning are published.

* * * *

Now WE see that, say, a silver salver or tray made and marked in London in 1544 AD would have the maker's mark, the leopard's head, a letter showing the date and the lion. A piece made today, over 400 years later, would have similar marks although the leopard's head would have lost its crown and, of course, the date letter would be different.

Now let us look at some actual marks. The photograph shows a silver fish knife on which you can just see some tiny stampings. The enlarged photograph lets us read them and we can see that the knife is sterling silver (the Lion); it was assayed in Sheffield (the Crown) in 1937 (from tables published by the Assay Office) and made by a silversmith who uses the initials AM. After this, you can have an interesting time finding out about any silver articles in your own home.

Of course, this is only part of the story but space prevents me telling you everything. For example, there is another standard known as 'Britannia' which has a special mark, and special marks were added, known as Commemorative Marks, for silver made in Jubilee years and for our Queen's coronation. Both Gold and Platinum have their particular Hall Marks, and gold and silver articles imported from other countries are given special marks. If you want to know more about this fascinating subject, you can do what I did, visit your local library and borrow books on Hall Marks — they are bound to have some.

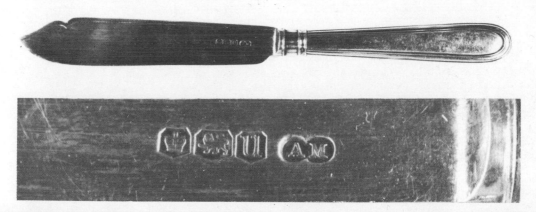

C	H	A	R	I	E	L	G	O
A	K	A	H	H	A	B	N	A
E	O	B	E	A	K	L	M	H
H	W	I	K	S	G	H	L	A
E	E	O	R	L	T	A	A	I

THE MISSING CHARACTER

This year's GREAT COMPETITION...

ALL SORTS OF SPORTS

What it's all about

No doubt you enjoy getting out-of-doors for a walk or run . . . to play with your friends . . . to take part in a sport. On the opposite page our artist, Martin Aitchison, has drawn people taking part in all sorts of sports. Look at them. Now . . .

Here's what you have to do . . .

1. Correctly identify each sport by writing the name of the sport alongside a particular drawing. We have done the CRICKET one for you (except for colouring it in) so that you can see what to do.
2. Colour in each panel with paints, crayons or felt tip pens.
3. Fill in the Entry Form at the bottom of the page.
4. Cut out the page neatly along the dotted line and send it, to arrive not later than 29th February 1980 to:

Cub Scout Annual Competition,
Baden-Powell House,
Queen's Gate,
LONDON SW7 5JS

The Rules

1. All competitors must be under the age of 11 years on 31st December 1979.
2. The closing date for the competition is 29th February 1980.
3. The entries will be judged for the following (in this order):
   a. the correct identification of the sports illustrated;
   b. the standard of colouring of the pictures, taking the age of the competitor into consideration.
4. The entry must be all the competitor's own work.
5. The Editor's decision is final. No correspondence can be entered into and entries cannot be returned. Prizewinners will be notified by post, and a full list of winners will be published in SCOUTING Magazine.

How to play THE NUMBERS GAME

On the board on the back cover of your Annual

The Numbers Game can be played by one to four players. The aim of the game is to move from the START, one square at a time, to the FINISH. Where there are two or more players, the one to reach FINISH first is the winner.

How to Play

* The numbers on the board are from 1 – 6. The game can be played with a dice; *or* a numbered spinner with six segments; or you can decide on any other way of getting the numbers 1, 2, 3, 4, 5, and 6 (for example, use a pack of cards, with the 7's, 8's, 9's, 10's, Jacks, Queens and Kings removed).
* Each player needs a small coloured disc or other object which he can move from square to square.

The Rules

1. All players' counters are placed at the START.
2. To decide who goes first, throw the dice, spin the spinner, etc. The player with the highest number has the first go.
3. A player can move only one square at a time, which must be the number of an adjacent square. A counter can be moved in any direction where there is a number (horizontally, vertically or diagonally).
4. If a player gets the number of an adjacent square he MUST move (even if it is backwards!), and he has another turn, and continues to have additional turns until he cannot move. The dice (or whatever) is then passed to the next player.
5. If a player gets a number and cannot move (this is when the number on the dice is not the same as any of the adjacent squares), he 'misses' the turn and the dice goes to the next player.
6. A square may be 'occupied' by the counters of more than one player.

60

All Sorts of Sports Competition Entry Form

PLEASE COMPLETE THE FORM IN BLOCK CAPITALS

drawings by Martin Aitchison

Name ~~Andrew Key~~ ANDREW KEY.

Address 120 LOVE LACE DRIVE
PYRFORD
WOKING
SURRY GU228RZ.

Cub Scout Pack (if any):
PYRFORD RED.

Date of birth 28/10/70.

Please complete this section as well: The three items which I most enjoyed in the 1980 Cub Scout Annual were:

1. _____
2. _____
3. _____

I would like to make these suggestions for items in a future Cub Scout Annual:

1. _____
2. _____

The 1981 Cub Scout Annual is being prepared!

Here are a few glimpes of what you will find . . .

The Butterfly Bush

A fascinating feature about the creatures which live in, or visit, the buddleia bush.

Eyes on Four Legs

Some Devon Cub Scouts find out how guide dogs for the blind are trained

Behind the scenes of **The Polka Children's Theatre**

Puzzles, Games and Teasers

```
        C
        R
        O
        S
W O R D S
```

Two stories set in 1916, to mark the 65th Birthday of Cub Scouting.

A Super Competition sponsored by British Rail

. . . and there'll be lots more in its packed pages.
So to avoid disappointment, make sure you are prepared!

ORDER YOUR COPY EARLY!